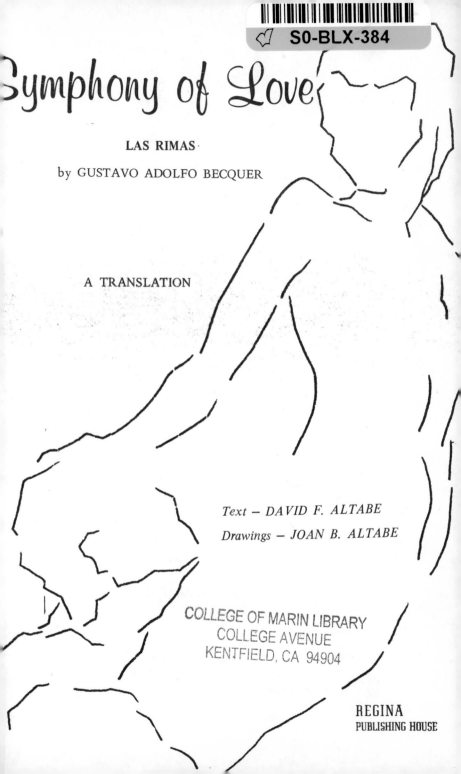

Symphony of Love

LAS RIMAS

by GUSTAVO ADOLFO BECQUER

A TRANSLATION

Text — *DAVID F. ALTABE*

Drawings — *JOAN B. ALTABE*

REGINA
PUBLISHING HOUSE

Library of Congress Catalog Card No. 73-91756

Printed in The United States of America

DEDICATION

My Dearest Joan

As these poems, which I dedicate to you, approach publication, my mind goes back to our honeymoon when on the back of a menu, I translated for you Rima 50 ("Today Heaven and Earth smile at Me"). Though they were Becquer's words, the sentiments were mine, and I could think of no more beautiful and appropriate verses to express the depth of my gratitude to you for becoming my wife.

My desire, in translating the Rimas, has been to share with you Becquer's inspiring thoughts and emo—tions, clothed as they are in apparent simplicity, but vibrant as a note plucked on a harp. It meant a lot to me to do so for in the Rimas, I had found the words that unlocked my innermost feelings.

Your drawings are a translation into line of Becquer's poetry, and so I know that you, too, have been inspired by him. Thus, this book is yours for so many reasons. May it be successful in leading others to know love.

David

CONTENTS

(The Roman numeral indicates the number of the Rima in the order traditionally assigned. The order followed in this edition is that given by Becquer in the <u>Libro de los gorriones</u>. For the convenience of those accustomed to the traditional arrangement of the Rimas, the following index is included.)

(The following Rimas do not form a part of the Libro de los gorriones, Becquer's original collection of the Rimas. They have been gathered by scholars, admirers of Becquer's work, and have been attributed to him. Most current editions of the Rimas usually include these poems.)

SYMPHONY OF LOVE

Text . . . . David F. Altabé

Drawings . . . . Joan B. Altabé

A translation into English verse of
Gustavo Adolfo Becquer's
RIMAS

Regina Publishing House
Long Beach, N.Y.

INTRODUCCION SINFONICA

In the dark corners of my mind, huddled together and unclothed, sleep the extravagant children of my imagination, waiting in silence for Art to dress them in words so that they may be able to present themselves decently on the world's stage.

Fertile, like the nuptial bed of Misery, and similar to those parents who beget more children than they can feed, my Muse conceives and gives birth in the mysterious sanctuary of my brain, populating it with innumerable creations for which neither my energy nor all the remaining years of my life would be sufficient to give them form.

And here within, naked and deformed, scrambled and jumbled together in indescribable confusion, I sometimes feel them stir and live with a dark and strange life, like that of those myriads of seeds which tremble and seethe in an eternal incubation within the entrails of the earth, without finding sufficient strength to come to the surface and be converted, at the kiss of the sun, into flowers and fruits.

With me they go, destined to die with me, without leaving a trace other than that which remains of a midnight dream which cannot be remembered in the morning. On some occasions, and in the presence of this frightening thought, there rises in them the will to live and, quaking in a terrifying though silent tumult, they seek in a throng a way to come to light from the darkness in which they dwell. But oh! between the world of ideas and that of form, there exists an abyss that only words can span, and words, timid and faltering, refuse to support their efforts. Mute, somber, and impotent, after the futile struggle, they fall once again into their old marasmus. If the wind stops, the withered leaves raised by the windstorm fall thus, motionless into the furrows of the paths.

These uprisings of the rebellious children of my imagination explain some of my fevers; they are the cause, unknown to science, of my elations and my depressions. And in this way, although poorly, I have been living until now: parading before the indifferent crowd, this silent tempest of my mind. I have been living thus, but there is an end to all things and these have to be put to an end.

Insomnia and Fantasy continue and they go on procreating in hideous union. Their creations, already cramped like feeble plants in a nursery, struggle to prolong their illusory existence, quarreling amongst themselves over the atoms of memory, as if it were the scarce water of a barren land. It is necessary to open a path to deeper waters which will eventually break the dike, waters fed daily by a running stream.

Go, then! Go and live with the only life I can give you! My intellect will feed you enough for you to be tangible. It will dress you, although it be in rags, adequately enough so that your nudity will not shame you. I would like to make for each of you a wondrous cloth woven of exquisite phrases in which you could wrap yourselves with pride as in a mantle of purple. I would like to be able to carve the form which is to contain you as one fashions a golden vial which is to hold a prized perfume. But it is impossible!

Nevertheless, I need to rest; I need; in the same way as the body is bled, the plethoric thrust of the blood surging through its swollen veins; to relieve the brain, no longer capable of containing so many absurdities.

Remain then deposited here, like the nebulous wake which marks the passing of an unknown comet: like the atoms dispersed from a world in embryo which death emits through the air before the creator has been able to pronounce the 'flat lux' which separates light from darkness.

I don't want you to return on sleepless nights and come before my eyes in an extravagant procession, begging with gestures and contorsions that I bring you forth to the life of reality from the limbo in which you live, like vaporous phantoms. When this old and worn out harp breaks, I don't want the unplayed notes it contained to be lost at the same time as the instrument. I wish to busy myself a bit with world that surrounds me, to be able to take my eyes away from this other world I carry in my brain, once it is empty. Common sense, which is the barrier to dreams, is beginning to weaken, and the peoples of both camps mix with one another and become confused. It takes effort on my part to distinguish between the things I have dreamed and those that have happened to me; my heart is divided between phantoms of my imagination and real people; my memory records the confused names and dates of women and days that have died or passed, with the days and women who have never existed except in my mind. It is necessary to end by casting you from my brain once and for all.

If to die is to sleep, I wish to sleep in peace in the night of death without your coming to be my nightmare, cursing me for having condemned you to nothingness before you were born. Go then to the world at whose contact you were engendered and remain in it like the echo which its joys and its sorrows, its hopes and its struggles, found in a soul which passed through the earth.

Perhaps very shortly, I will have to pack my suitcase for the great journey; from one hour to the next, the spirit may free itself from the flesh in order to rise to purer regions. I do not wish, when this happens, to take with me, like the motley baggage of a mountebank, the treasure of tinsel and tatters which my imagination has been accumulating in the attic of my brain.

All are architects of Fate,
    Working in these walls of Time;
Some with massive deeds and great,
    Some with ornaments of rhyme.

(Longfellow, "The Builders")

LAS   RIMAS

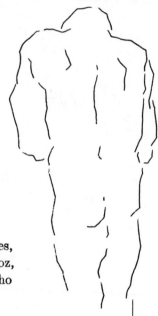

A Elisa

Para que los leas con tus ojos grises,
para que los cantes con tu clara voz,
para que llenen de emoción tu pecho
hice mis versos yo.

Para que encuentren en tu pecho asilo
y les des juventud, vida, calor,
tres cosas que yo no puedo darles,
hice mis versos yo.

Para hacerte gozar con mi alegría,
para que sufras tú con mi dolor,
para que sientas palpitar mi vida,
hice mis versos yo.

Para poder poner ante tus plantas
la ofrenda de mi vida y de mi amor,
con alma, sueños rotos, risas, lágrimas,
hice mis versos yo.

To Elisa

For you to read it with your grey eyes,
For your clear voice to sing its words,
For your heart to be filled with sighs,
I wrote my verse.

For it to find asylum in your breast,
For your youth, life, and warmth to nurse,
Three things I can no longer express,
I wrote my verse.

For you to rejoice in my elation,
For you to suffer with my hurts,
For you to feel my life's palpitation,
I wrote my verse.

To be able to place before your feet
This offering of my love and life's works,
With soul, laughter, tears, and broken dreams,
I wrote my verse.

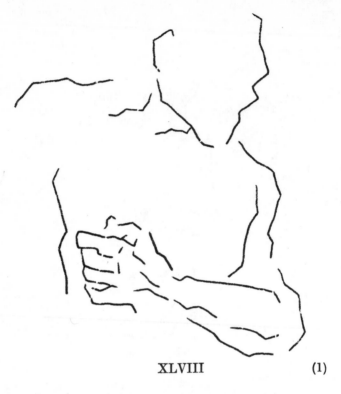

XLVIII   (1)

Como se arranca el hierro de una herida
su amor de las entrañas me arranqué,
aunque sentí al hacerlo que la vida
me arrancaba con él!

Del altar que le alcé en el alma mía
la voluntad su imagen arrojó,
y la luz de la fe que en ella ardía
ante el ara desierta se apagó.

Aun para combatir mi firme empeño
viene a mi mente su visión tenaz...
¡Cuándo podré dormir con ese sueño
en que acaba el soñar!!

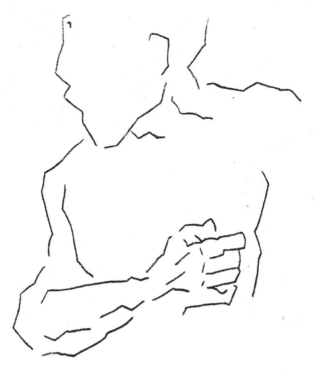

1 (XLVIII)

Like steel is torn from a wound,
Her love from within me I tore,
Although I felt, as I did so, doomed;
My life uprooted in the steel I bore.

The sacred image which I had raised
Of her, from my heart I cast,
And before the altar, the light of faith
In her which burned, burnt its last.

Still, over my firm resolve creeps
A vision of her everseen . . .
When will I be able to sleep
That sleep which ends all dreams!

XLVII   (2)

Yo me he asomado a las profundas simas
de la tierra y del cielo,
y les he visto el fin, o con los ojos,
o con el pensamiento.

Mas ay! de un corazón llegué al abismo
y me incliné un momento,
y mi alma y mis ojos se turbaron:
¡Tan hondo era y tan negro!!

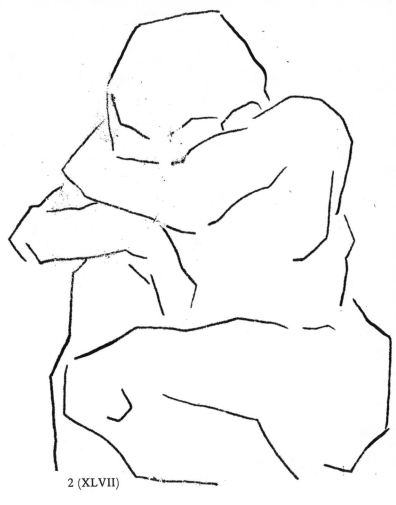

2 (XLVII)

I have peered into the deep
Caverns of earth and skies;
I've seen their depth with my eyes
Or in my thoughts and dreams.

But Oh! The abyss of a heart I reached
And for a moment I inclined,
And my eyes and my soul went blind:
It was so black and deep.

En la clave del arco mal seguro
cuyas piedras el tiempo enrojeció,
obra de cincel rudo campeaba
el gótico blasón.

Penacho de su yelmo de granito,
la yedra que colgaba en derredor
daba sombra al escudo en que una mano
tenía un corazón.

A contemplarle en la desierta plaza
nos paramos los dos:
Y, ése, me dijo, es el cabal emblema
de mi constante amor.

Ay! es verdad lo que me dijo entonces:
verdad que el corazón
lo llevará en la mano... en cualquier parte...
pero en el pecho no.

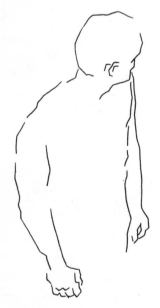

3 (XLV)

On the keystone of an unsteady arch,
On whose face a crude chisel had pressed,
And time had reddened, there stood apart
An Heraldic crest.

Of the granite helmet, its plumed part
Was the ivy which around it fell;
It shaded the shield on which a heart
In a hand was held.

To contemplate it, in the deserted square,
We stopped; and raising her head,
"That stands, that emblem you see there,
For my eternal love," she said.

Oh, 'tis true that her heart,
As she then expressed,
She carries in her hand, or any part,
But not in her breast.

Los suspiros son aire y van al aire!
Las lágrimas son agua y van al mar!
Dime, mujer, cuando el amor se olvida
¿sabes tú adónde va?

4 (XXXVIII)

Sighs are breaths and rise in the air;
Tears are water and to the sea they flow.
Tell me, woman, when love is forgotten,
Where does it go?

PRIMERA VOZ

Las ondas tienen vaga armonía,
las vïoletas suave olor,
brumas de plata la noche fría,
luz y oro el día,
5 yo algo mejor;
yo tengo *Amor!*

SEGUNDA VOZ

Aura de aplausos, nube radiosa,
ola de envidia que besa el pie,
isla de sueños donde reposa
10 el alma ansiosa,
dulce embriaguez
la *Gloria* es!

TERCERA VOZ

Ascua encendida es el tesoro,
sombra que huye la vanidad.
Todo es mentira: la gloria, el oro,
lo que yo adoro
sólo es verdad;
la *Libertad!*

Así los barqueros pasaban cantando
la eterna canción
y al golpe del remo saltaba la espuma
y heríala el sol.

—¿Te embarcas? gritaban, y yo sonriendo
les dije al pasar:
Yo ya me he embarcado; por señas que aún tengo
la ropa en la playa tendida a secar.

First Voice

The waves have a vague, harmonic roll;
Violets, a fragrance sublime;
A silvery mist, the night cold;
The day, light and gold;
I have something more divine;
Love is mine!

Second Voice
The aura of applause, a radiant breeze,
Waves of envy which kiss,
An isle of dreams to which the anxious soul flees
And rest at ease,
Inebriate bliss
Glory is this!

Third Voice
Treasure is a live coal,
Vanity, a shadow that fades with rapidity,
All is illusion: the glory, the gold,
Truth is all I hold
Of any validity;
Liberty!

Thus passed the mariners chanting
The song eternally sung,
And their oars set the foam splashing
And it was struck by the sun.

"Are you coming aboard?" they shouted, and I, smiling
As they passed, called back hard:
' My clothes stretched on the beach drying
Are proof that I've already embarked."

Fatigada del baile,
encendido el color, breve el aliento,
apoyada en mi brazo
del salón se detuvo en un extremo.

Entre la leve gasa
que levantaba el palpitante seno,
una flor se mecía
en compasado y dulce movimiento.

Como en cuna de nácar
que empuja el mar y que acaricia el céfiro
tal vez allí dormía
al soplo de sus labios entreabiertos.

Oh! quién así, pensaba,
dejar pudiera deslizarse el tiempo!
Oh! si las flores duermen,
¡qué dulcísimo sueño!

6 (XVIII)

Tired from the dance,
Her color heightened, short of breath,
Leaning on my arm,
Into a corner of the room we stepped.

Midst the flimsy silk
Which rose on her heaving breast,
A flower rocked
In rhythmic movement blessed.

Cradled in mother of pearl
Which the wind and seas caress,
Fanned by her half opened lips,
There it peacefully slept.

"Oh, who, I mused, "in that way,
Could deliciously let time slip away!
Oh, if flowers sleep,
What heavenly dreams!"

XXVI (7)

Voy contra mi interés al confesarlo,
no obstante, amada mía,
pienso cual tú que una oda sólo es buena
de un billete del Banco al dorso escrita.
No faltará algún necio que al oirlo
se haga cruces y diga:
Mujer al fin del siglo diez y nueve
material y prosaica... Boberías!
Voces que hacen correr cuatro poetas
que en invierno se embozan con la lira!
Ladridos de los perros a la luna!
Tú sabes y yo sé que en esta vida
con genio es muy contado el que *la escribe*
y con oro cualquiera *hace* poesía.

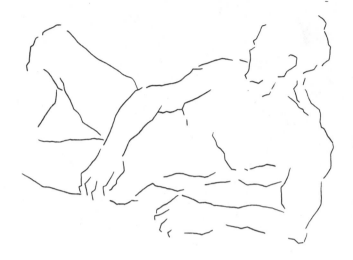

7 (XXVI)

I go against my concern to confess,
My beloved, ———still,
I think as you, that a poem is only good
When written on the back of a dollar bill.
No doubt, there'll be some fool who hearing this,
Cross himself and babble, he will,
"Woman at Nineteeth Century's end
Materialistic and dull.   . " What swill!
Words spread by poets who in wintertime,
Muffle themselves in their sonnets against the chill
The howling of dogs at the moon!
You and I know that in this life; with skill
And genius there are few who write poetry;
But make up rhymes, for money, anyone will.

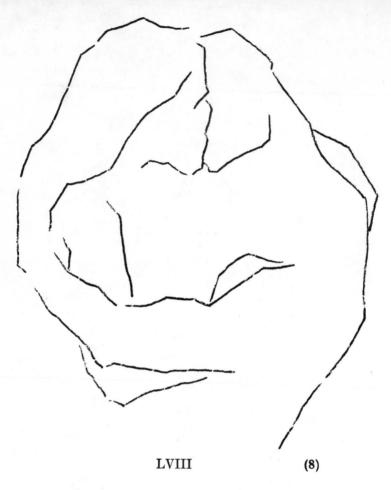

LVIII

¿Quieres que de ese néctar delicioso
no te amargue la hez?
Pues aspírale, acércale a tus labios
y déjale después.

¿Quieres que conservemos una dulce
memoria de este amor?
Pues amémonos hoy mucho y mañana
digámonos, adiós!

8 (LVIII)

Do you wish to preserve the essence
Of that delicious nectar?
Breathe it, bring it to your lips shut tight
And then, set it aside.

Do you wish a sweet remembrance
Of this love to remain forever?
Then let's love each other tonight
And tomorrow, say good—bye!

LV (9)

Entre el discorde estruendo de la orgía
acarició mi oído
como nota de música lejana
el eco de un suspiro.

El eco de un suspiro que conozco,
formado de un aliento que he bebido,
perfume de una flor que oculta crece
en un claustro sombrío.

Mi adorada de un día, cariñosa
—¿En qué piensas? me dijo:
—En nada... —En nada ¿y lloras? —Es que tengo
alegre la tristeza y triste el vino.

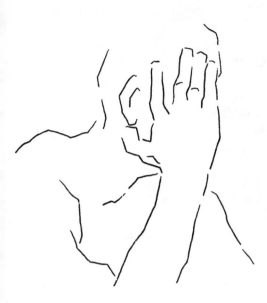

9 (LV)

Midst the dissonant din of the orgy
There reached my ear,
Like the notes of some distant music
The echo of a tear.

The echo of a sigh familiar,
Formed by a breath that once breathed near,
The perfume of a flower growing hidden
In the shadow of a cloistered garden's rear.

My beloved for a day asked affectionately,
"What are you thinking of, my dear?"
"Nothing."———"Nothing, and you're crying?"
——"I find joy in sadness, and sadness
                              in all this beer."

Como en un libro abierto
leo de tus pupilas en el fondo;
¿A qué fingir el labio
risas que se desmienten con los ojos?

Llora! No te avergüences
de confesar que me quisiste un poco.
Llora! Nadie nos mira.
Ya ves; yo soy un hombre... y también lloro.

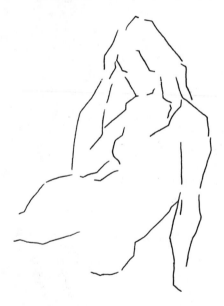

10 (XLIV)

Like an open book
I read the depth of your eyes;
Why feign with your lips
Laughter which your eyes deny?

Cry! Do not be ashamed to confess
That your love for me painfully dies.
Cry! No one is looking at us.
You see, I am a man and I, too, cry.

Yo sé un himno gigante y extraño
que anuncia en la noche del alma una aurora,
y estas páginas son de ese himno
cadencias que el aire dilata en las sombras.

Yo quisiera escribirle, del hombre
domando el rebelde mezquino idïoma,
con palabras que fuesen a un tiempo
suspiros y risas, colores y notas.

Pero en vano es luchar; que no hay cifra
capaz de encerrarle, y apenas ¡oh hermosa!
si teniendo en mis manos las tuyas
pudiera al oído cantártelo a solas.

11 (I)

I know a hymn gigantic and strange
Which brings dawn to the soul's night,
And these pages are of that hymn
Cadences which in shadows soar in flight.

I would like to write it, of man
Mastering words rebellious and remote,
With words which are at one time
Sighs and laughter, colors and notes.

But the struggle is in vain; there is no key
Capable of containing it, and hardly my dear,
If holding your hands in mine,
I could sing it in your ear.

Lo que el salvaje que con torpe mano
hace de un tronco a su capricho un dios
y luego ante su obra se arrodilla,
eso hicimos tú y yo.

Dimos formas reales a un fantasma
de la mente ridícula invención
y hecho el ídolo ya, sacrificamos
en su altar nuestro amor.

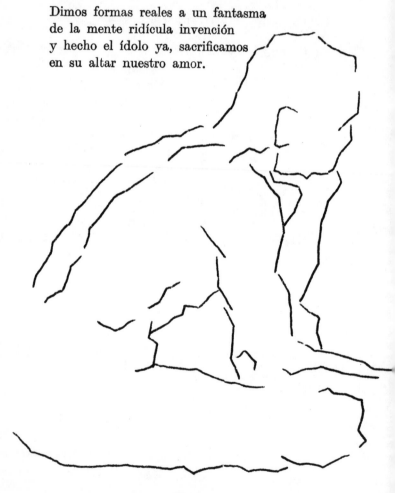

12 (L)

Like savages who with primitive hands
Make of a tree trunk gods on high,
And then kneel to worship their work,
This we did, you and I.

We gave living forms to a phantom,
A foolish invention of the mind,
And once the idol was fashioned,
On its altar, we left our love to die.

Del salón en el ángulo oscuro,
de su dueña tal vez olvidada,
silenciosa y cubierta de polvo,
veíase el arpa.

¡Cuánta nota dormía en sus cuerdas
como el pájaro duerme en las ramas,
esperando la mano de nieve
que sabe arrancarlas!

Ay! pensé; ¡cuántas veces el genio
así duerme en el fondo del alma
y una voz como Lázaro espera
que le diga «Levántate y anda!»

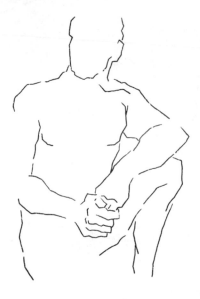

13 (VII)

By its master perhaps forgotten,
Standing in a corner dark,
Covered with dust and silent,
One could see a harp.

How many notes lay there sleeping
In its strings like a nested bird,
Awaiting a skilled white hand to play it
In order to be heard!

Oh, I thought; how often genius
Sleeping thus, in the soul, lies,
Awaiting, like Lazarus, a voice
To command it, "Arise!"

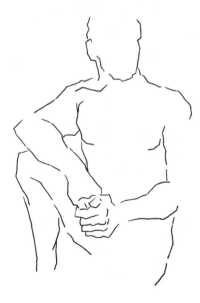

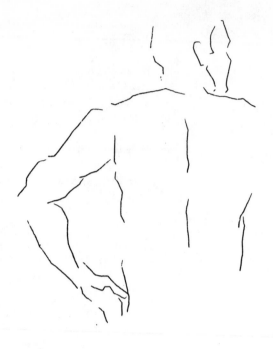

XLIX (14)

Alguna vez la encuentro por el mundo
y pasa junto a mí:
y pasa sonriéndose y yo digo
¿Cómo puede reir?

Luego asoma a mi labio otra sonrisa
máscara del dolor,
y entonces pienso: —Acaso ella se ríe,
como me río yo.

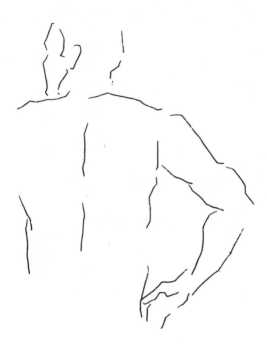

14 (XLIX)

Sometimes I meet her along the way
And she crosses my path:
And passes smiling, and I say,
"How can she laugh?"

Then another smile crosses my lips,
A mask of pain,
And then I think, "Perhaps her laugh
 s like mine, a smile feigned."

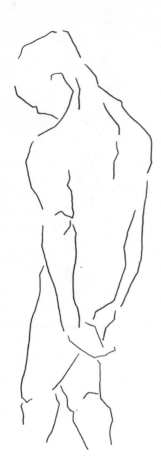

Saeta que voladora
cruza arrojada al azar,
y que no se sabe donde
temblando se clavará;

Hoja que del árbol seca
arrebata el vendaval,
sin que nadie acierte el surco
donde al polvo volverá;

Gigante ola que el viento
riza y empuja en el mar,
y rueda y pasa, y se ignora
qué playa buscando va.

Luz que en cercos temblorosos
brilla próxima a expirar
y que no se sabe de ellos
cuál el último será.

Eso soy yo que al acaso
cruzo el mundo sin pensar
de donde vengo ni a donde
mis pasos me llevarán.

15 (II)

An arrow flying cross the air,
Cast off by a careless hand,
And no one knows where
Trembling it will stand;

A dry leaf windswept
From off its branch,
Without anyone guessing
The rut where it will land;

A giant wave which the wind
At sea curls and fans,
Which rolls and passes searching
for some unknown strand;

Light about to fade,
Which shines in flickering bands,
All wondering which of them
To shine will be the last;

This am I, who wanders
Through the world without a plan,
Without thinking of where
I'm destined, nor of my past.

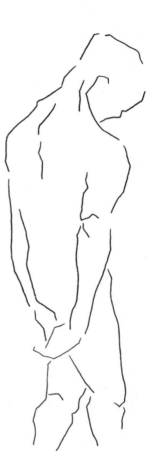

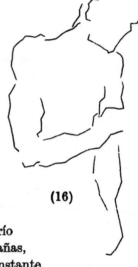

XLII (16)

Cuando me lo contaron sentí el frío
de una hoja de acero en las entrañas,
me apoyé contra el muro, y un instante
la conciencia perdí de donde estaba.

Cayó sobre mi espíritu la noche,
en ira y en piedad se anegó el alma
y entonces comprendí por qué se llora!
y entonces comprendí por qué se mata!

Pasó la nube de dolor... con pena
logré balbucear breves palabras...
¿quién me dio la noticia?... Un fiel amigo...
Me hacía un gran favor... Le di las gracias.

16 (XLII)

When they told me, I felt the cold
Of a blade of steel run me through.
I rested against a wall, and for a moment,
I knew not where I was nor what to do.

Night fell on my spirit;
My soul drowned as anger and self pity grew.
And then I understood why one shed tears!
And then I understood why one slew!

The cloud of pain passed;
I found some useless words and muttered a few.
Who was it who told me? A faithful friend . . .
He did me a favor . . . I gave him the thanks due.

Yo sé cuál el objeto
de tus suspiros es,
yo conozco la causa de tu dulce
secreta languidez.
Te ríes?... Algún día
sabrás, niña, por qué.
Tú acaso lo sospechas,
    y yo lo sé.

Yo sé cuando tú sueñas,
y lo que en sueños ves,
como en un libro, puedo, lo que callas
en tu frente leer.

Te ríes?... Algún día
sabrás, niña, por qué.
Tú acaso lo sospechas,
    y yo lo sé.

Yo sé por qué sonríes
y lloras a la vez:
yo penetro en los senos misteriosos
de tu alma de mujer.
Te ríes?... Algún día
sabrás, niña, por qué;
mientras tú sientes mucho y nada sabe
yo, que no siento ya, todo lo sé.

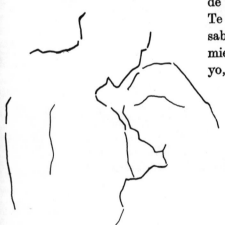

17 (LIX)

I know the hidden
Object of your sigh;
Your secret languor——
I know the reason why.
You laugh? . . . Someday,
My child, you'll understand;
You . . . hardly suspect why it is so,
And I . . . I know.

I know when you dream
And what in dreams you behold;
I read on your forehead
What your lips leave untold.
You laugh? . . . Someday,
My child, you'll understand;
You . . . hardly suspect why it is so,
And I . . . I know.

I know why you smile
And cry in the same breath,
I penetrate your womanly soul
To its mysterious depth.
You laugh? . . . Someday
My child, you'll understand;
While you feel much and nothing know,
I, who feel no longer, know it so . .

LXVII (18)

¡Qué hermoso es ver el día
coronado de fuego levantarse,
y a su beso de lumbre
brillar las olas y encenderse el aire!

¡Qué hermoso es tras la lluvia
del triste Otoño en la azulada tarde,
de las húmedas flores
el perfume aspirar hasta saciarse!

¡Qué hermoso es cuando en copos
la blanca nieve silenciosa cae,
de las inquietas llamas
ver las rojizas lenguas agitarse!

Qué hermoso es cuando hay sueño
dormir bien... y roncar como un sochantre...
y comer... y engordar... ¡y qué fortuna
que esto sólo no baste!

18 (LXVII)

How beautiful it is to see the day
Crowned with fire arise
And with the kiss of its rays
Burn the sea and ignite the skies!

How beautiful it is, on afternoons
In autumn, after the rains' chill,
To breathe the fragrant perfume
Of damp flowers to one's fill!

How beautiful it is, when white snow
Is falling heavily in wintry silent air,
To see the flickering red tongues
Of a restless fire, rise and flare.

How beautiful it is, when strength is drained,
To sleep like a deacon and snore and puff,
And to eat, and grow fat, and —— Oh, how sad,
That all this is not enough!

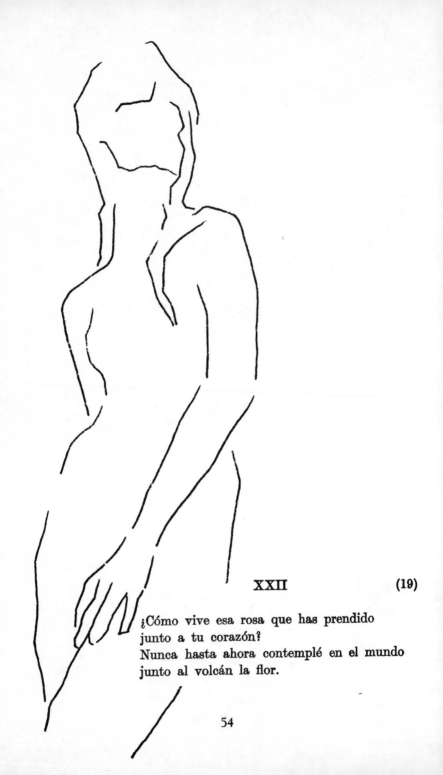

XXII   (19)

¿Cómo vive esa rosa que has prendido
junto a tu corazón?
Nunca hasta ahora contemplé en el mundo
junto al volcán la flor.

54

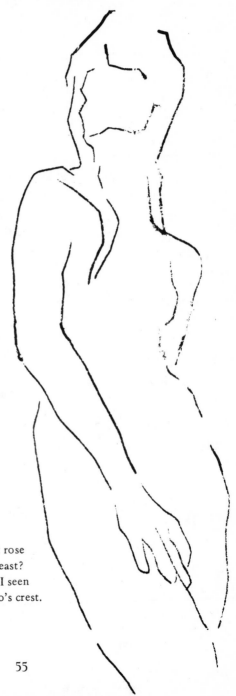

19 (XXII)

How does it live, that rose
You wear on your breast?
Never, till now, have I seen
A flower on a volcano's crest.

Hoy como ayer, mañana como hoy,
y siempre igual!
Un cielo gris, un horizonte eterno
y andar... andar.

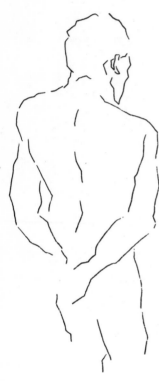

Moviéndose a compás como una estúpida
máquina el corazón:
la torpe inteligencia del cerebro
dormida en un rincón.

El alma, que ambiciona un paraíso,
buscándole sin fe.
Fatiga sin objeto, ola que rueda
ignorando por qué.

Voz que incesante con el mismo tono
canta el mismo cantar.
Gota de agua monótona que cae
y cae sin cesar.

Así van deslizándose los días
unos de otros en pos,
hoy lo mismo que ayer... y todos ellos
sin gozo ni dolor.

Ay! a veces me acuerdo suspirando
del antiguo sufrir!
¡Amargo es el dolor; pero siquiera
padecer es vivir!

20 (LVI)

Today like yesterday, tomorrow like today,
And always, always the same!
A gray sky, an endless horizon,
And rambling without aim.

The heart like a stupid machine ticking,
Keeping its steady beat;
The intelligence of a sluggish brain,
In a corner, asleep.

The soul, disillusioned and without faith,
Searching for the sky;
Senseless weariness, a wave that flows
Without knowing why.

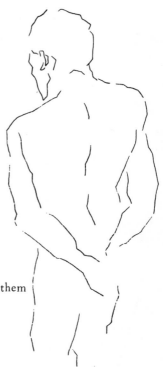

An incessant voice in a monotone
Chanting the same song;
A steady flow of water that drips,
And drips, and drips along.

Thus, one after the other,
Pass the days;
Today, the same as yesterday . . . and all of them
Without pleasure or pain.

Oh! sometimes I remember sighing,
The suffering I did!
Pain is bitter, but even
To suffer is to live!

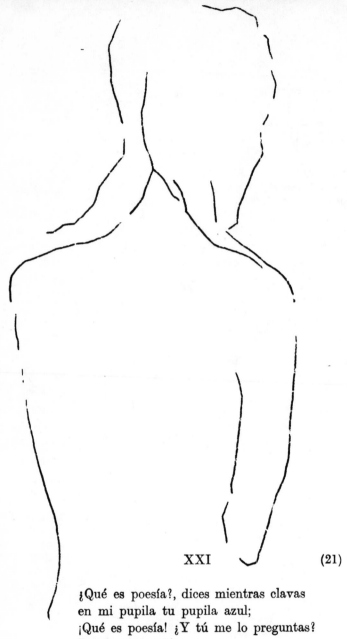

XXI   (21)

¿Qué es poesía?, dices mientras clavas
en mi pupila tu pupila azul;
¡Qué es poesía! ¿Y tú me lo preguntas?
Poesía... eres tú.

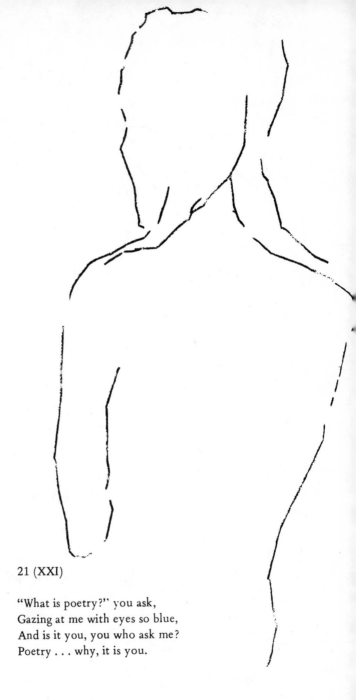

21 (XXI)

"What is poetry?" you ask,
Gazing at me with eyes so blue,
And is it you, you who ask me?
Poetry . . . why, it is you.

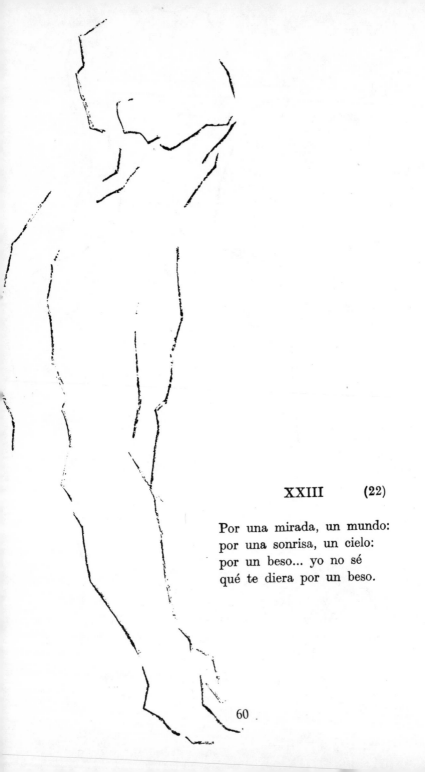

XXIII (22)

Por una mirada, un mundo:
por una sonrisa, un cielo:
por un beso... yo no sé
qué te diera por un beso.

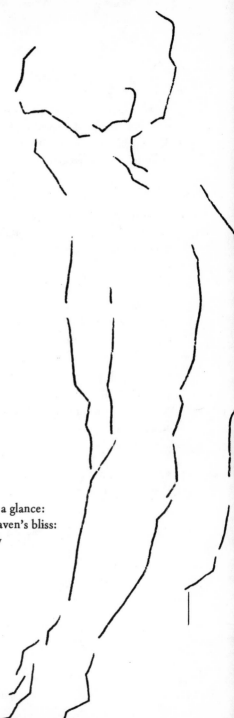

22 (XXXIII)

I'd give the world for only a glance:
For one of your smiles, heaven's bliss:
For a kiss . . . I don't know
What I'd give for a kiss.

61

¿Será verdad que cuando toca el sueño
con sus dedos de rosa nuestros ojos,
de la cárcel que habita huye el espíritu
en vuelo presuroso?

¿Será verdad que huésped de las nieblas,
de la brisa nocturna al tenue soplo,
alado sube a la región vacía
a encontrarse con otros?

¿Y allí desnudo de la humana forma,
allí los lazos terrenales rotos,
breves horas habita de la idea
el mundo silencioso?

¿Y ríe y llora y aborrece y ama
y guarda un rastro del dolor y el gozo,
semejante al que deja cuando cruza
el cielo un meteoro?

Yo no sé si ese mundo de visiones
vive fuera o va dentro de nosotros:
Pero sé que conozco a muchas gentes
a quienes no conozco.

23 LXXV)

Is it true that when sleep
With its rosy fingers touches our eyes,
The spirit from the prison it inhabits
Hastily flies?

Is it true that as the clouds' guest,
Upon the thin breath of the night breeze,
It climbs to meet others in the empty air
On invisible wings?

And there, stripped of human form
After casting off its earthly bowers,
It lives in the silent world of ideas
For a few brief hours?

And it laughs and it cries, hates and loves,
And keeps a trace of pain and delight,
Similar to a meteor when it crosses
The sky at night?

I don't know if that world of visions
Lives within us or without, above or below;
But I know that I know many people
Whom I do not know.

Las ropas desceñidas,
desnudas las espadas,
en el dintel de oro de la puerta
dos ángeles velaban.

Me aproximé a los hierros
que defienden la entrada,
y de las dobles rejas en el fondo
la vi confusa y blanca.

La vi como la imagen
que en leve ensueño pasa,
como rayo de luz tenue y difuso
que entre tinieblas nada.

Me sentí de un ardiente
deseo llena el alma;
como atrae un abismo, aquel misterio
hacia sí me arrastraba.

Mas ay! que de los ángeles
parecían decirme las miradas
—El umbral de esta puerta
sólo Dios lo traspasa.

24 (LXXIV)

Their clothes ungirded,
Their swords drawn,
Two angels kept vigil
On the gilded lintel of the door.

I approached the entrance
Railing of iron wrought,
And beyond the double grillwork,
Vague and pale, a girl I saw.

I saw her like an image
Which light dreams spawn,
Like a soft ray of light swimming,
Diffused in shadows long.

I felt my soul filled
With an eerie desire warm;
Like to an abyss, to that mystery,
I was relentlessly drawn.

But Oh! It seemed the angels
Said by their glance and sword,
"The threshold of this portal
Can only be crossed by the Lord."

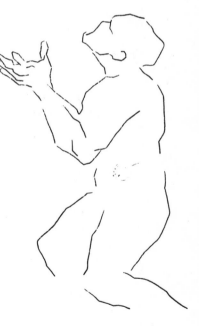

Cuando miro el azul horizonte
perderse a lo lejos,
al través de una gasa de polvo
dorado e inquieto;
me parece posible arrancarme
del mísero suelo
y flotar con la niebla dorada
en átomos leves
cual ella deshecho!

Cuando miro de noche en el fondo
oscuro del cielo
las estrellas temblar como ardientes
pupilas de fuego;
me parece posible a do brillan
subir en un vuelo
y anegarme en su luz, y con ellas
en lumbre encendido
fundirme en un beso.

En el mar de la duda en que bogo
ni aún sé lo que creo;
sin embargo estas ansias me dicen
que yo llevo algo
divino aquí dentro.

25 (VIII)

When I look at the blue horizon
Fading in the dusk
Through a wavering gauze
Speckled with golden dust,
It seems possible to tear myself
From the earth's lowly crust,
And float with the gilded mist
On light atoms,
Likewise untrussed.

When I look at the dark
Depth of the skies at night,
At the stars trembling
Like pupils burning bright,
It seems possible for me
To where they're shining, rise in flight
And drown in their light and with them
In a burning,
Flaming kiss ignite.

In the sea of doubt in which I float,
I'm not sure of my beliefs.
These longings tell me, nevertheless,
That something divine
Within me seethes.

Tú eras el huracán y yo la alta
torre que desafía su poder:
tenías que estrellarte o que abatirme!...
¡No pudo ser!

Tú eras el oceano y yo la enhiesta
roca que firme aguarda su vaivén:
tenías que romperte o que arrancarme!...
¡No pudo ser!

Hermosa tú, yo altivo: acostumbrados
uno a arrollar, el otro a no ceder:
la senda estrecha, inevitable el choque...
¡No pudo ser!

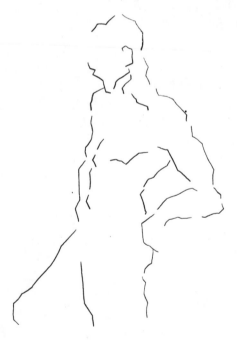

26 (XLI)

You were the hurricane and I,
A tall tower which challenges the sea:
You had to break or I crumble ..
It couldn't be!

You were the ocean and I, a jutting
Rock which awaits its beat:
You had to break or I crumble . . .
I couldn't be!

You, beautiful; I, haughty; accustomed,
One to captivate and the other not to cede:
The road was narrow, the clash inevitable . . .
It couldn't be!

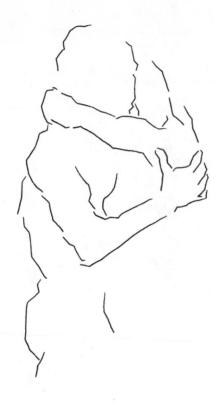

IX (27)

Besa el aura que gime blandamente
las leves ondas que jugando riza,
el sol besa a la nube en occidente
y de púrpura y oro la matiza,
la llama en derredor del tronco ardiente
por besar a otra llama se desliza
y hasta el sauce inclinándose a su peso
al río que le besa, vuelve un beso.

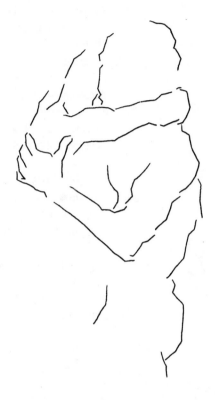

27 (IX)

The dawn which softly howls
Kisses the waves it playfully curls;
The sun kisses the western clouds
Whose purple and gold it unfurls;
A flame around a burning trunk
To kiss another slips;
And even the willow, bending under its bulk
To the river which kisses it, returns a kiss.

Antes que tú me moriré: escondido
en las entrañas ya
el hierro llevo con que abrió tu man
la ancha herida mortal.

Antes que tú me moriré: y mi espíritu
en su empeño tenaz
se sentará a las puertas de la muerte,
esperándote allá.

Con las horas los días, con los días
los años volarán,
y a aquella puerta llamarás al cabo...
¿Quién deja de llamar?

Entonces que tu culpa y tus despojos
la tierra guardará,
lavándote en las ondas de la muerte
como en otro Jordán:

Allí donde el murmullo de la vida
temblando a morir va,
como la ola que a la playa viene
silenciosa a expirar:

Allí donde el sepulcro que se cierra
abre una eternidad,
Todo cuanto los dos hemos callado
allí lo hemos de hablar.

28 (XXXVII)

I will die before you;
And hidden in the earth's womb,
I will bear the steel with which
You opened my mortal wound.

I will die before you;
And my soul with anxious breath,
Seated there will await you
Before the gates of death.

With the hours, the days, and days
With the years will fly,
And at last, you will call at that door . . .
In the end, everyone must die.

Then the earth will keep
Your sins and your remains;
Like another Jordan, death
Will wash you in its waves.

There, where the ripples of life
Trembling sink into the mire;
Like the surf comes upon a beach,
Silently to expire,

There, where eternity opens
To all things that are dead,
We shall speak you and I
Of all that we left unsaid.

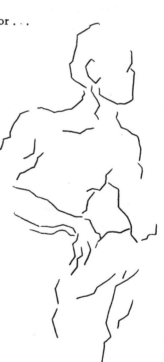

XIII   (29)

Tu pupila es azul, y cuando ríes
su claridad suave me recuerda
el trémulo fulgor de la mañana
que en el mar se refleja.

Tu pupila es azul y cuando lloras
las transparentes lágrimas en ella
se me figuran gotas de rocío
sobre una vïoleta.

Tu pupila es azul y si en su fondo
como un punto de luz radia una idea
me parece en el cielo de la tarde
una perdida estrella.

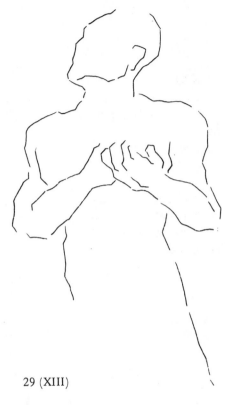

29 (XIII)

Your eyes are blue and when you laugh,
They remind me so clear and soft
Of the dawn's tremulous fire
Sent by the sea aloft.

Your eyes are blue and when you weep
The transparent tears on your eyelids
Seem to me like dewdrops
Shed on violets.

Your eyes are blue and, if from their depth,
An idea should, like a flash of light, arise,
To me it's like a lost star
In the afternoon skies.

Nuestra pasión fue un trágico sainete
en cuya absurda fábula
lo cómico y lo grave confundidos
risas y llanto arrancan.

Pero fue lo peor de aquella historia
que al fin de la jornada
a ella tocaron lágrimas y risas
y a mí, sólo las lágrimas.

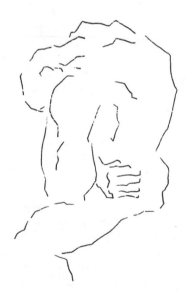

30 (XXXI)

Our passion was a tragic farce
In whose absurd acts,
Comedy with tragedy combined
Plucked both tears and laughs.

But the worst part of it all
Was that when the lights went on,
She was left with tears and laughter,
But all my laughter was gone.

Cuando en la noche te envuelven
las alas de tul del sueño
y tus tendidas pestañas
semejan arcos de ébano,
por escuchar los latidos
de tu corazón inquieto
y reclinar tu dormida
cabeza sobre mi pecho,
diera, alma mía,
cuanto poseo,
la luz, el aire
y el pensamiento!

Cuando se clavan tus ojos
en un invisible objeto
y tus labios ilumina
de una sonrisa el reflejo,
por leer sobre tu frente
el callado pensamiento
que pasa como la nube
del mar sobre el ancho espejo,
diera, alma mía,
cuanto deseo,
la fama, el oro,
la gloria, el genio!

Cuando enmudece tu lengua
y se apresura tu aliento
y tus mejillas se encienden
y entornas tus ojos negros,
por ver entre sus pestañas
brillar con húmedo fuego
la ardiente chispa que brota
del volcán de los deseos,
diera, alma mía,
por cuanto espero,
la fe, el espíritu,
la tierra, el cielo.

31 (XXV)

When night enfolds you
In sleep's tulle arms,
And your eyelashes in repose
Seem like ebony arcs,
To listen to the beat
Of your restless heart,
And lay upon my chest
Your head sleeping calm,
    I would give, my beloved,
    All that is mine:
    Light and air
    And thoughts divine!

When your eyes are fixed
Upon some object unseen,
And by its light, a shadow
Of a smile on your lips appears,
To read on your forehead
Thoughts silent, but not serene
That pass like clouds
Mirrored on distant seas,
    I would give, my beloved,
    All I desire:
    Gold, fame, glory,
    And inspiration's fire.

When your tongue is mute,
And you breathe in haste,
Your eyes half closed
And your cheeks ablaze,
To see between your lashes
Burning with humid flame
The ardent spark that spurts
From the volcano of passions insane,
    I would give, my beloved
    For what I await,
    Heaven and earth,
    My soul and my faith.

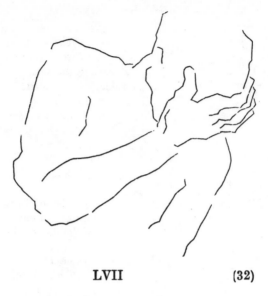

LVII (32)

Este armazón de huesos y pellejo
de pasear una cabeza loca
se halla cansado al fin y no lo extraño
pues aunque es la verdad que no soy viejo,

de la parte de vida que me toca
en la vida del mundo, por mi daño
he hecho un uso tal, que juraría
que he condensado un siglo en cada día.

Así, aunque ahora muriera,
no podría decir que no he vivido;
que el sayo al parecer nuevo por fuera,
conozco que por dentro ha envejecido.

Ha envejecido, sí; pese a mi estrella!
harto lo dice ya mi afán doliente;
que hay dolor que al pasar, su horrible huella
graba en el corazón, si no en la frente.

32 (LVII)

This hulk of hide and bones
Weighed down by a heavy mind
Maddened by insane cares
Is weary of its load,

This portion of life that's mine
Has seen so much, I'd swear . . .
Such suffering, so many tears
That each day seems like a hundred years.

So, if I should go now to my grave,
I've seen my share of life.
This garment that I wear is aged;
Though it may look new, it's worn inside.

I've aged, yes; whatever my fate!
My sickened soul is scarred
By a pain that shows not on the face,
But leaves its lines etched on the heart.

81

Dos rojas lenguas de fuego
que a un mismo tronco enlazadas
se aproximan, y al besarse
forman una sola llama;

Dos notas que del laúd
a un tiempo la mano arranca,
y en el espacio se encuentran
y armoniosas se abrazan;

Dos olas que vienen juntas
a morir sobre una playa
y que al romper se coronan
con un penacho de plata;

Dos jirones de vapor
que del lago se levantan
y al juntarse allá en el cielo
forman una nube blanca;

Dos ideas que al par brotan,
dos besos que a un tiempo estallan,
dos ecos que se confunden,
eso son nuestras dos almas.

33 (XXIV)

Two red tongues of fire
Around a log embrace,
Come close, and kiss,
And form a single flame;

Two notes of a lute,
Plucked at the same time,
Meet each other in space,
And harmoniously chime;

Two waves, together come
Upon a beach to rest,
And breaking are crowned
With one silvery crest;

Two streaks of mist
From the same lake rise,
And on joining, form
A single cloud in the skies;

Two ideas which at one time surge,
Two pairs of lips which simultaneously kiss,
Two echoes which merge . . .
Our two souls are this.

Dejé la luz a un lado, y en el borde
de la revuelta cama me senté,
mudo, sombrío, la pupila inmóvil
clavada en la pared.

Qué tiempo estuve así? No sé: al dejarme
la embriaguez horrible de[l] dolor,
expiraba la luz y en mis balcones
reía el sol.

Ni sé tampoco en tan terribles horas
en qué pensaba o qué pasó por mí;
sólo recuerdo que lloré y maldije
y que en aquella noche envejecí.

34 (XLIII)

I left the light to one side and sat
On the edge of the turned down bed;
Mute and somber and immobile,
My eyes stared straight ahead.

How long did I stay so? I don't know.
When the drunken horror of my shock
Left me, the light was flickering its last
And on my balcony, the sun was hot.

Nor do I know what I thought
As those terrible hours raged;
I only remember that I cried and cursed,
And that on that night, I aged.

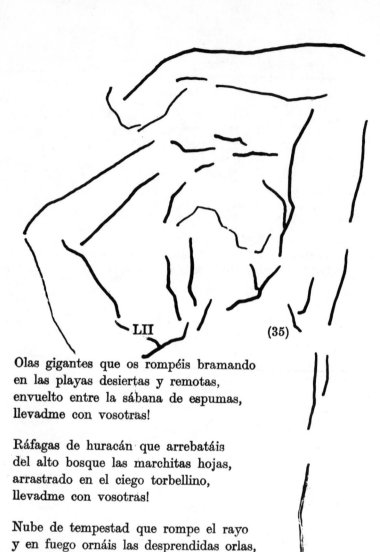

LII (35)

Olas gigantes que os rompéis bramando
en las playas desiertas y remotas,
envuelto entre la sábana de espumas,
llevadme con vosotras!

Ráfagas de huracán que arrebatáis
del alto bosque las marchitas hojas,
arrastrado en el ciego torbellino,
llevadme con vosotras!

Nube de tempestad que rompe el rayo
y en fuego ornáis las desprendidas orlas,
arrebatado entre la niebla oscura,
llevadme con vosotras!

Llevadme por piedad a donde el vértigo
con la razón me arranque la memoria.
Por piedad! tengo miedo de quedarme
con mi dolor a solas!

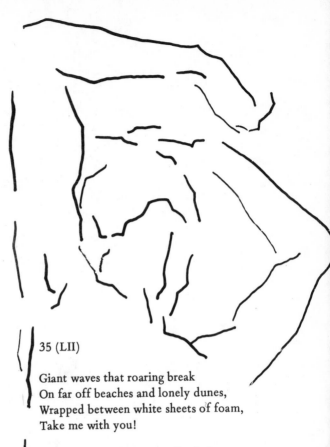

35 (LII)

Giant waves that roaring break
On far off beaches and lonely dunes,
Wrapped between white sheets of foam,
Take me with you!

Hurricane winds that blindly shake
Forest trees, trunk and root,
And carry off withered leaves,
Take me with you!

Storm clouds split by lightning rays
And blanketed in fiery hues,
Swept up in the blackened fog,
Take me with you!

Take me, Oh please, for mercy's sake
Where memories scatter in the whirlwind's brew.
I'm afraid to remain alone with my pain;
For mercy's sake, take me with you!

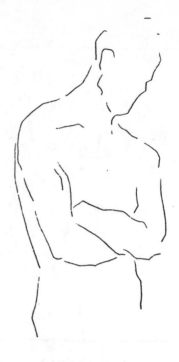

LIV (36)

Cuando volvemos las fugaces horas
del pasado a evocar,
temblando brilla en sus pestañas negras
una lágrima pronta a resbalar.

Y al fin resbala y cae como gota
de rocío al pensar
que cual hoy por ayer, por hoy mañana
volveremos los dos a suspirar.

36 (LIV)

When we recall
The fleeting hours of the past,
A tear, trembling and about to fall,
Hovers, and at last

Slips from her eyes like dew
On thinking that as we cry this way
For yesterday, tomorrow, too
We will sigh for today.

XX   (37)

Sabe si alguna vez tus labios rojos
quema invisible atmósfera abrazada,
que el alma que hablar puede con los ojos
también puede besar con la mirada.

37 (XX)

Know, that if ever the invisible air
Burning sears your ruby lips,
That the soul that speaks through stares,
Can also, with a glance, kiss.

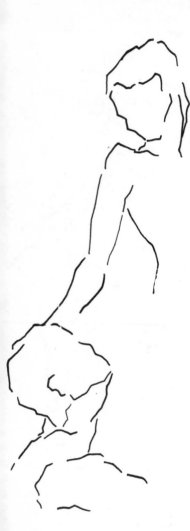

Volverán las oscuras golondrinas
en tu balcón sus nidos a colgar,
y otra vez con el ala a sus cristales
jugando llamarán.

Pero aquellas que el vuelo refrenaban
tu hermosura y mi dicha a contemplar,
aquellas que aprendieron nuestros nombre
ésas... no volverán!

Volverán las tupidas madreselvas
de tu jardín las tapias a escalar
y otra vez a la tarde aún más hermosa
sus flores se abrirán.

Pero aquellas cuajadas de rocío
cuyas gotas mirábamos temblar
y caer como lágrimas del día...
ésas... no volverán!

Volverán del amor en tus oídos
las palabras ardientes a sonar,
tu corazón de su profundo sueño
tal vez despertará.

Pero mudo y absorto y de rodillas
como se adora a Dios ante su altar,
como yo te he querido... desengáñate,
nadie así te amará.

(LIII)

ce again, dark swallows will appear
your terrace to build their nests,
d playfully fold their wings
d come to rest,

t those who halted in flight
gaze upon your beauty and my gain,
ose who learned our names,
ose . . . never again!

nce again, the thick honeysuckle
ill, your garden walls, caress,
nd on afternoons still more beautiful,
are their blossoms fresh,

t those dampened by the morning dew
hose drops, like tears of day's pain,
e watched tremble and fall,
hose . . . .Never again!

nce again, with ardent words of love,
ou will be addressed.
erhaps it will awaken that heart
lumbering within your breast,

t mute, kneeling, and absorbed,
s when prayers, on God's altar, are lain,
s I have loved you . . Do not be deceived,
ike that . . . never again!

93

No digáis que agotado su tesoro
de asuntos falta enmudeció la lira:
podrá no haber poetas; pero siempre
habrá poesía.

Mientras las ondas de la luz al beso
palpiten encendidas,
mientras el sol las desgarradas nubes
de fuego y oro vista,
mientras el aire en su regazo lleve
perfumes y armonías,
mientras haya en el mundo primavera,
habrá poesía!

Mientras la ciencia a descubrir no alcance
las fuentes de la vida,
y en el mar o en el cielo haya un abismo
que al cálculo resista,
mientras la humanidad siempre avanzando
no sepa a do camina,
mientras haya un misterio para el hombre,
habrá poesía!

Mientras se sienta que se ríe el alma,
sin que los labios rían;
mientras se llore, sin que el llanto acuda
a nublar la pupila;
mientras el corazón y la cabeza
batallando prosigan,
mientras haya esperanzas y recuerdos,
habrá poesía!

Mientras haya unos ojos que reflejen
los ojos que los miran,
mientras responda el labio suspirando
al labio que suspira,
mientras sentirse puedan en un beso
dos almas confundidas,
mientras exista una mujer hermosa
habrá poesía!

39 (IV)

Don't say, that, lacking thoughts,
The poet's lyre has ceased to ring:
Poets may cease to exist, but
Poetry, there'll always be.

So long as waves of light
Palpitate at a kiss with desire,
So long as the sun dresses the clouds
With hues of gold and fire,

So long as the air carries in its lap
Fragrant perfumes and harmony:
So long as the world has spring,
Poetry, there'll always be!

So long as science fails to discover
Why we live and why we die,
And calculus cannot fathom
The depths of sea and sky,

So long as humanity in its advance,
Its destination cannot see,
So long as there remain a mystery to man,
Poetry, there'll always be!

So long as the soul feels joy
Which a laugh does not reveal,
As long as tears do not descry
The sadness on may feel,

So long as heart and mind
In endless conflict seethe,
So long as there be memory and hope,
Poetry, there'll always be!

So long as eyes can reflect
The look in another's eyes,
So long as lips respond
With sighs to another's sighs,

So long as a kiss can unite
Two souls for all eternity,
So long as there are beautiful women
Poetry, there'll always be!

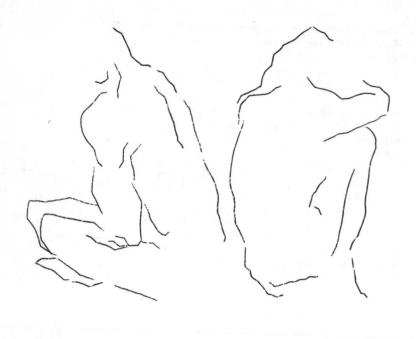

XXX

Asomaba a sus ojos una lágrima
y a mi labio una frase de perdón;
habló el orgullo y se enjugó su llanto,
y la frase en mis labios expiró.

Yo voy por un camino: ella, por otro;
pero al pensar en nuestro mutuo amor,
yo digo aún ¿por qué callé aquel día?
Y ella dirá ¿por qué no lloré yo?

40 (XXX)

A tear on her eyelids appeared,
And on my lips a pardoning word,
But pride spoke and she dried her tears,
And from my lips, nothing was heard.

I went one way; she went another;
But thinking back on when we were lovers,
I ask, "why did I let the words die?"
And she must ask, "why didn't I cry?"

LX (41)

Mi vida es un erial,
flor que toco se deshoja;
que en mi camino fatal
alguien va sembrando el mal
para que yo lo recoja.

41 (LX)

My life is a barren waste of weeds,
Each flower that I touch withers;
For in this life that I lead,
Someone goes planting an evil seed
So that I may pick it.

Sacudimiento extraño
que agita las ideas
como huracán que empuja
las olas en tropel.

Murmullo que en el alma
se eleva y va creciendo
como volcán que sordo
anuncia que va a arder.

Deformes siluetas
de seres imposibles,
paisajes que aparecen
como al través de un tul,

Colores que fundiéndose
remedan en el aire
los átomos del Iris
que nadan en la luz,

Ideas sin palabras,
palabras sin sentido,
cadencias que no tienen
ni ritmo ni compás,

Memorias y deseos
de cosas que no existen,
accesos de alegría,
impulsos de llorar,

Actividad nerviosa
que no halla en qué emplearse
sin riendas que le guíe
caballo volador,

Locura que el espíritu
exalta y desfallece,
embriaguez divina
del genio creador

Tal es la inspiración.

Gigante voz que el caos
ordena en el cerebro
y entre las sombras hace
la luz aparecer,

Brillante rienda de oro
que poderosa enfrena
de la exaltada mente
el volador corcel,

Hilo de luz que en haces
los pensamientos ata,
sol que las nubes rompe
y toca en el zenit,

Inteligente mano
que en un collar de perlas
consigue las indóciles
palabras reunir,

Armonioso ritmo
que con cadencia y número
las fugitivas notas
encierra en el compás,

Cincel que el bloque muerde
la estatua modelando,
y la belleza plástica
añade a la ideal,

Atmósfera en que giran
con orden las ideas
cual átomos que agrupa
recóndita atracción,

Raudal en cuyas ondas
su sed la fiebre apaga,
Oasis que al espíritu
devuelve su vigor.

Tal es nuestra razón.

Con ambas siempre en lucha,
y de ambas vencedor
tan sólo al genio es dado
a un yugo atar las dos.

A strange tremor
Which stirs ideas,
Like a hurricane pushing
The waves in a whirl;

A murmur which in the soul
Rises and keeps growing
Like a still volcano's
Prelude to the lava it will hurl;

Deformed silhouettes
Of impossible beings;
Vague landscapes
Through tulle unfurled;

Colors which fusing
Copy in the air,
The atoms of the rainbow
Swimming in light's heat;

Ideas without words,
Words without sense,
Cadences which lack
Rhythm or beat;

Memories and desires
Of non–existant things,
Outbursts of joy,
Impulses of tears;

Nervous activity
Which finds no use,
A flying horse with no one
To pull the reins in;

A madness which exalts
And weakens the soul,
A creative genius'
Divine intoxication . . .

Such is inspiration.

An imperious voice
Which orients the mind's
Chaos, and in the shadows,
Makes light appear;

Brilliant bridle of gold
Which powerfully reins
The excited mind's
Flying steed;

A thread of light which
Binds thoughts into sheaves,
A sun breaking through the clouds
And touching heights;

A dexterous hand
Which into strings of pearls
Brings indocile words
Together to unite;

A harmonious rhythm
Which in cadence and numbers
Encloses straying notes
Into a beat;

A chisel which bites the block,
Modeling a statue,
And adds plastic beauty
To an ideal;

An atmosphere in which ideas
Revolve in order,
Like molecules where atoms
Join through attraction unseen,

A stream in whose waves
Fever's thirst is abated;
An oasis which renews vigor
To the soul's lesions . . .

Such is reason.

With both always in conflict,
And master of them both,
Only the genius can tie the two
To one yoke.

XVI (43)

Si al mecer las azules campanillas
de tu balcón,
crees que suspirando pasa el viento
murmurador,
sabe que oculto entre las verdes hojas
suspiro yo.

Si al resonar confuso a tus espaldas
vago rumor,
crees que por tu nombre te ha llamado
lejana voz,
sabe que entre las sombras que te cercan
te llamo yo.

Si se turba medroso en la alta noche
tu corazón,
al sentir en tus labios un aliento
abrasador,
sabe que aunque invisible al lado tuyo
respiro yo.

43 (XVI)

If when on your balcony, you hear bellflowers
        seem to weave,
That it's the whispering wind's passing murmur,
        you believe,
Know that it is I sighing, hiding
        among the green leaves.

If behind you, in a vague, confused whisper,
        you should hear
Your name being called by a voice distant
        and unclear,
Know that it is I in the shadows which surround you,
        standing near.

If, in the depth of night, your heart so timid
        skips a beat,
On feeling on your lips a breath burning
        with passion's heat;
Know that it is I panting at your side
        unseen.

LXXVII

(44)

Dices que tienes corazón, y sólo
lo dices porque sientes sus latidos;
eso no es corazón... es una máquina
que al compás que se mueve hace ruido.

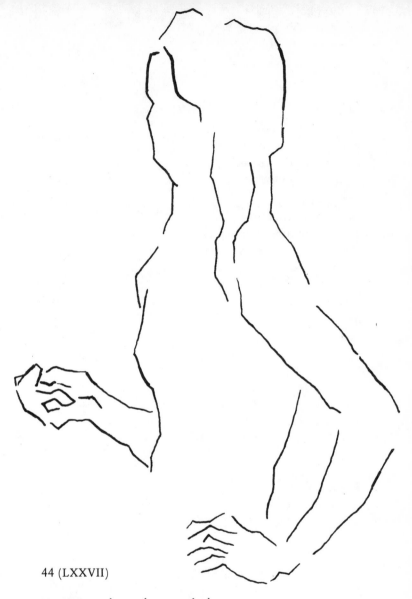

44 (LXXVII)

You say you have a heart, and why;
Only because you feel it beat.
That's not a heart . . . It has a rhythm
And makes noise, but it's only a machine.

Al ver mis horas de fiebre
e insomnio lentas pasar,
a la orilla de mi lecho,
¿quién se sentará?

Cuando la trémula mano
tienda próximo a expirar
buscando una mano amiga,
¿quién la estrechará?

Cuando la muerte vidríe
de mis ojos el cristal,
mis párpados aún abiertos
¿quién los cerrará?

Cuando la campana suene
(si suena en mi funeral)
una oración al oírla
¿quién murmurará?

Cuando mis pálidos restos
oprima la tierra ya,
sobre la olvidada fosa
¿quién vendrá a llorar?

¿Quién en fin al otro día
cuando el sol vuelva a brillar
de que pasé por el mundo
¿quién se acordará?

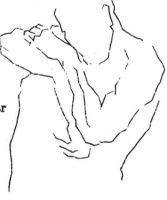

45 (LXI)

On seeing my hours of fever
And sleeplessness slowly tread,
Who will come to sit
At the edge of my lonely bed?

When close to death,
A trembling hand I extend,
Searching for a hand to hold,
Who will be there? What friend?

When death will glaze
My eyes, yet unclosed,
Who will turn down the lids
To their final repose?

When (if at my funeral)
Churchbells peal,
To mumble a prayer,
Who will stop and kneel?

When dust will cover
My weary bones,
Who will come to cry
Over the forgotten stone?

And on the following day,
When the sun will shine again
        in all its splendor,
That I have been on this earth,
Who will remember?

X   (46)

Los invisibles átomos del aire
en derredor palpitan y se inflaman,
el cielo se deshace en rayos de oro,
la tierra se estremece alborozada,
oigo flotando en olas de armonías
rumor de besos y batir de alas,
mis párpados se cierran... Qué sucede?
—Es el amor que pasa!

46 (X)

The invisible atoms of air
Pulsate around me in flames;
The sky shatters into golden rays,
The earth trembles with glee;
I hear floating in harmonious waves,
The murmur of kisses and beating of wings;
My eyes close . . . What are these things?
——It's love going by!

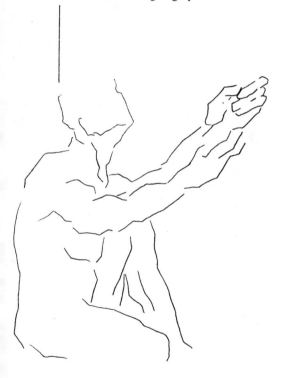

LXV   (47)

Llegó la noche y no encontré un asilo
y tuve sed!... mis lágrimas bebí;
y tuve hambre! Los hinchados ojos
cerré para morir!

Estaba en un desierto? Aunque a mi oído
de las turbas llegaba el ronco hervir
yo era huérfano y pobre... el mundo estaba
desierto... para mí!

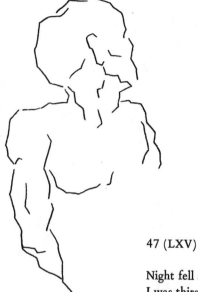

47 (LXV)

Night fell and I found no refuge;
I was thirsty! . . . I drank my tears;
I was hungry! I closed my swollen eyes
Awaiting death's release!

I was in a desert! Yet I could
Hear the raucous mob seethe.
I was an orphan and poor . . . the world
Was deserted . . . for me!

Fingiendo realidades
con sombra vana,
delante del Deseo
va la Esperanza.

Y sus mentiras
como el Fénix renacen
de sus cenizas.

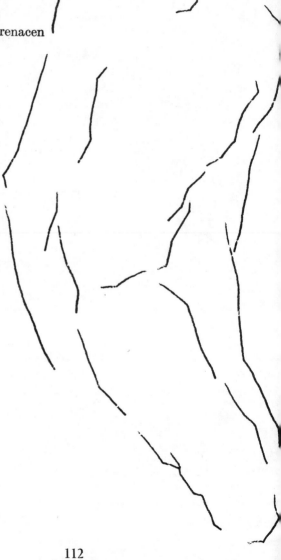

48 (LXXVIII)

Feigning reality,
In the flame of Desire,
With shadowy vanity,
Hope is inspired.

And its lies,
From the ashes,
Like the Phoenix rise.

113

Al brillar de un relámpago nacemos
y aún dura su fulgor cuando morimos;
¡tan corto es el vivir!

La gloria y el amor tras que corremos
sombras de un sueño son que perseguimos;
¡despertar es morir!

49 (LXIX)

In a flash of lightning, we are born;
Its light still shines when we are through;
How short is life!

The glory and love for which we long
Are shadows of a dream that we pursue;
To awaken is to die!

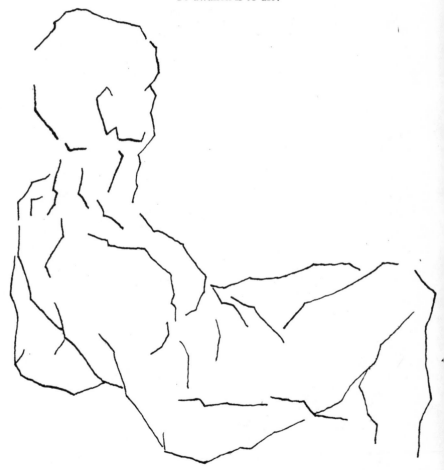

XVII   (50)

Hoy la tierra y los cielos me sonríen,
hoy llega al fondo de mi alma el sol,
hoy la he visto... la he visto y me ha mirado...
hoy creo en Dios!

50 (XVII)

Today Heaven and Earth smile at me;
Today the Sun reaches the bottom of my heart;
Today I saw her .. I saw her and she looked at me ...
Today I believe in God!

XI   (51)

—Yo soy ardiente, yo soy morena,
yo soy el símbolo de la pasión,
de ansia de goces mi alma está llena:
A mí me buscas?
                    —No es a tí: no.

—Mi frente es pálida, mis trenzas de oro:
puedo brindarte dichas sin fin,
yo de ternuras guardo un tesoro
A mí me llamas?
                    —No: no es a tí.

—Yo soy un sueño, un imposible,
vano fantasma de niebla y luz
soy incorpórea, soy intangible:
no puedo amarte:
                    —¡Oh ven; ven tú!

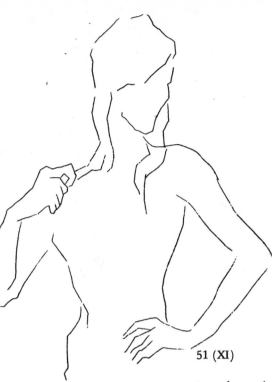

51 (XI)

I am the symbol of passion,
Dark and fiery as the sun;
My soul is full of ardent desires;
Are you looking for me?
        ——No, you're not the one.

My skin is fair, my hair, blond;
To you, with tenderness I come;
I can offer eternal bliss;
Are you calling me?
        ——No you're not the one.

I am an impossible dream,
I am the incorporate, the intangible one;
A vague phantom of shadow and light;
I cannot love you.
        ——Oh, come, come, come!

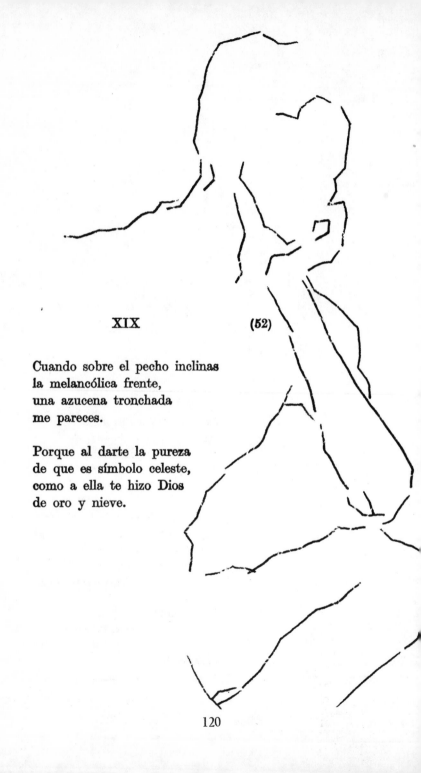

XIX   (52)

Cuando sobre el pecho inclinas
la melancólica frente,
una azucena tronchada
me pareces.

Porque al darte la pureza
de que es símbolo celeste,
como a ella te hizo Dios
de oro y nieve.

52 (XIX)

When on your breast,
Your melancholy head you lean,
So like a freshly cut lily
You seem.

For on giving you the purity
For which the lily stands,
God made you as He made the flower,
Of gold and snowy strands.

La bocca mi baccio tutto tremante.

Sobre la falda tenía
el libro abierto,
en mi mejilla tocaban
sus rizos negros:
no veíamos las letras
ninguno creo,
mas guardábamos ambos
hondo silencio.
¿Cuánto duró? Ni aún entonces
pude saberlo.
Sólo sé que no se oía
más que el aliento,
que apresurado escapaba
del labio seco.
Sólo sé que nos volvimos
los dos a un tiempo,
y nuestros ojos se hallaron
y sonó un beso!

. . . .

. . . .

Creación de Dante era el libro,
era su Infierno,
cuando a él bajamos los ojos
yo dije trémulo:
¿Comprendes ya que un poema
cabe en un verso?
y ella respondió encendida
—Ya lo comprendo!

53 (XXIX)

She held an open book
        upon her knees.
Her black curls brushed
        against my cheek;
The letters, we saw
        not one, I believe,
But between us we kept
        a silence deep.
How long did it last? Even then
        I could not perceive.

Only her breath could be heard
        in that moment of bliss,
Which rushing escaped
        from her dry lips.
We turned towards each other,
        I remember this,
And our eyes met, and there was a sound,
        the sound of a kiss.

. . . .
. . . .

The book was the "Inferno" of Dante,
His masterpiece of divine woe.
When our eyes looked down upon it,
I, trembling, whispered low,
"Now do you understand how from one line,
And entire poem can grow?"
And she replied all aglow,
"Yes, I know!"

123

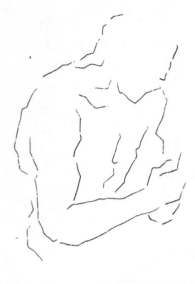

XXXVI   (54)

Si de nuestros agravios en un libro
se escribiese la historia,
y se borrase en nuestras almas cuanto
se borrase en sus hojas;

Te quiero tanto aún: dejó en mi pecho
tu amor huellas tan hondas,
que sólo con que tú borrases una,
las borraba yo todas!

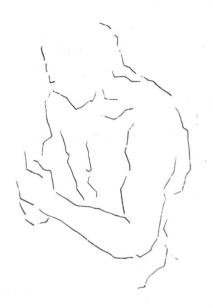

54 (XXXVI)

If in a book, the tale
Of our hurts were told,
And we could erase from its pages
Those imprinted on our souls,

I love you still so much,
You left in my heart traces so profound,
That if you were to erase but one,
None of mine would be found.

Una mujer me ha envenenado el alma,
otra mujer me ha envenenado el cuerpo;
ninguna de las dos vino a buscarme,
yo de ninguna de las dos me quejo.

Como el mundo es redondo, el mundo rueda.
Si mañana, rodando, este veneno
envenena a su vez ¿por qué acusarme?
¿Puedo dar más de lo que a mí me dieron?

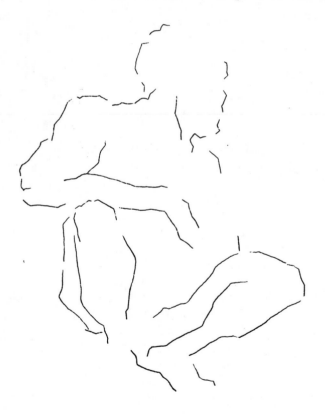

55 (LXXIX)

One woman poisoned my soul,
Another did my body profane,
Neither one came to look for me,
I, of neither one, complain.

But the world is round and it turns.
If tomorrow, with poison driven,
I poison in turn, why accuse me?
Can I give more than I've been given?

Primero es un albor trémulo y vago
raya de inquieta luz que corta el mar
luego chispea y crece y se dilata
en ardiente explosión de claridad.

La brilladora lumbre es la alegría,
la temerosa sombra es el pesar:
¡Ay en la oscura noche de mi alma
cuándo amanecerá?

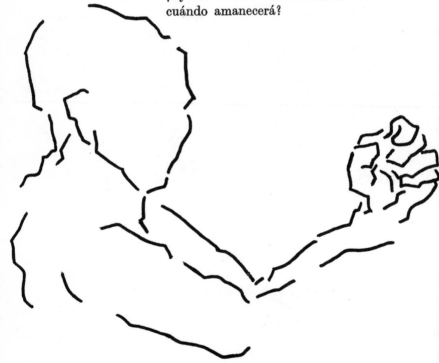

56 (LXII)

First it's a shimmering dawn and vague,
A ray of restless light cutting the ocean,
Then it sparkles, grows, and dilates
Into a flaming noon explosion.

The shining light is delight;
The fearsome shadow is sorrow:
Oh! In my soul's dark night,
When will it be morrow?

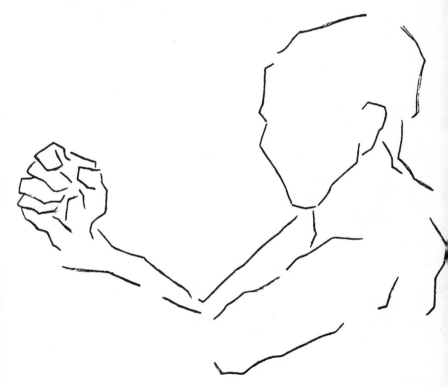

VI   (57)

Como la brisa que la sangre orea
sobre el oscuro campo de batalla,
cargada de perfumes y armonías
en el silencio de la noche vaga;

Símbolo del dolor y la ternura,
del bardo inglés en el horrible drama,
la dulce Ofelia, la razón perdida,
cogiendo flores y cantando pasa.

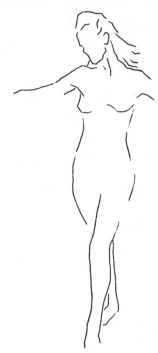

57 (VI)

Like a blood fed breeze drifting
O'er a dark and dank field of battle,
Bearing perfumes and harmonies,
She roams in the silence of night's mantle;

A symbol of pain and tenderness
In the awesome play, Hamlet,
The fair Ophelia, her reason gone,
Gathering flowers and   singing, passes.

XXVIII   (58)

Cuando entre la sombra oscura
perdida una voz murmura
turbando su triste calma,
si en el fondo de mi alma
la oigo dulce resonar;

Dime: ¿Es que el viento en sus giros
se queja, o que tus suspiros
me hablan de amor al pasar?

Cuando el sol en mi ventana
rojo brilla a la mañana,
y mi amor tu sombra evoca,
si en mi boca de otra boca
sentir creo la impresión;

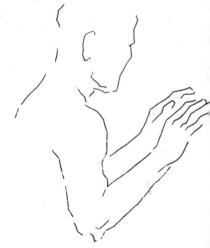

Dime: ¿es que ciego deliro,
o que un beso en un suspiro
me envía tu corazón?

Y en el luminoso día,
y en la alta noche sombría,
si en todo cuanto rodea
al alma que te desea
te creo sentir y ver;

Dime: ¿es que toco y respiro
soñando, o que en un suspiro
me das tu aliento a beber?

58 (XXVIII)

When lost in shadows dark,
Breaking the somber calm,
A voice whispers low;
If, deep in my soul,
I hear it sweetly resound;

Tell me, is it the wind passing by
Plaintively, or is it your sigh
Speaking to me of love profound?

When the sun on my windowpanes,
In the morning, shines in crimson flames,
And my love, your image divines;
If, from other lips on mine,
I seem to feel a mark;

Tell me, am I out of my mind,
Or is it that a kiss in a sigh
Is being sent to me by your heart?

If in the day's broad light,
And in the shadows of deep night,
If in all that's surrounding
This heart you set pounding,
I feel you and see you, I think;

Tell me, is all I feel and breathe
A dream, or that the sigh you heave
Brings me your breath to drink?

¡Cuántas veces al pie de las musgosas
paredes que la guardan,
oí la esquila que al mediar la noche
a los maitines llama!

¡Cuántas veces trazó mi triste sombra
la luna plateada
junto a la del ciprés que de su huerto
se asoma por las tapias!

Cuando en sombras la iglesia se envolvía,
de su ojiva calada
cuántas veces temblar sobre los vidrios
vi el fulgor de la lámpara!

Aunque el viento en los ángulos oscuros
de la torre silbara,
del coro entre las voces percibía
su voz vibrante y clara.

En las noches de invierno si un medroso
por la desierta plaza
se atrevía a cruzar, al divisarme
el paso aceleraba.

Y no faltó una vieja que en el torno
dijese a la mañana,
que de algún sacristán muerto en pecado
acaso era yo el alma.

A oscuras conocía los rincones
del atrio y la portada;
de mis pies las ortigas que allí crecen
las huellas tal vez guardan.

Los búhos que espantados me seguían
con sus ojos de llamas,
llegaron a mirarme con el tiempo
como a un buen camarada.

A mi lado sin miedo los reptiles
se movían a rastras,
hasta los mudos santos de granito
creo que me saludaban!

59 (LXX)

How many times, at the foot of the moss
Covered walls standing there,
Have I heard the tinkle of bells at midnight
Call the faithful to morning prayer!

How many times did the moon's silver
Sketch my sad shadow tall
Next to that of the cypresses
O'erhanging the garden wall!

When the church was draped in shade,
How many times did I see the dark
Illuminated by light trembling
On the windows of its pointed arch!

Although the wind whistled and howled
In the dark angles of its spire,
I could hear her voice clear and vibrant
Midst the mingled voices of the choir.

On winter nights, if some timid soul
Ventured across the deserted square,
He'd quicken his steps
On seeing me there.

And more than one old woman
In the morning, would begin
Saying that I was the soul perhaps
Of some sacristan who died in sin.

Of the threshold and the portal,
I knew every inch of space;
My footsteps perhaps are printed
In the nettle growing at its base.

The frightened owls who followed me
With their eyes burning red,
Came in time to look on me
As a comrade and a friend.

At my side, the reptiles moved,
Dragging themselves unperturbed,
And even the mute saints of granite
Greeted me, I observed.

135

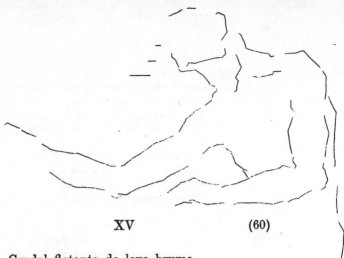

XV   (60)

Cendal flotante de leve bruma,
rizada cinta de blanca espuma,
rumor sonoro
de arpa de oro,
beso del aura, onda de luz,
       eso eres tú.

Tu sombra aérea que cuantas veces
voy a tocarte te desvaneces.
Como la llama, como el sonido,
como la niebla, como el gemido
       del lago azul!

En mar sin playas onda sonante,
en el vacío cometa errante,
largo lamento
del ronco viento,
ansia perpetua de algo mejor,
       eso soy yo.

Yo, que a tus ojos en mi agonía
los ojos vuelvo de noche y día;
yo, que incansable corro y demente
tras una sombra, tras la hija ardiente
de una visión!

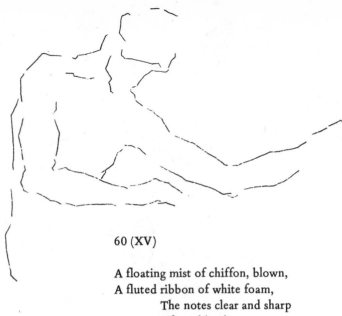

60 (XV)

A floating mist of chiffon, blown,
A fluted ribbon of white foam,
    The notes clear and sharp
    Of a golden harp,
A wave of light, the kiss of a breeze,
    You are these.

To my touch you disappear,
Whenever, ethereal shadow, I near,
    Like the flame, like the tone,
    Like the fog, like the moan
    Of the lake green!

On a beachless sea, a raging wave,
In space, a wandering ray,
    A long, lamenting dirge
    Of the wind's whining surge,
Filled with anxious hope evergreen,
    This is what I seem.

I, who in my agony, turn your way
My eyes from night to day;
I, who run untiringly and blindly
After a shadow, after the fiery
    Daughter of a dream!

LXVIII   (61)

No sé lo que he soñado
en la noche pasada.
Triste muy triste debió ser el sueño
pues despierto la angustia me duraba.

Noté al incorporarme
húmeda la almohada,
y por primera [vez] sentí al notarlo
de un amargo placer henchirse el alma.

Triste cosa es el sueño
que llanto nos arranca,
mas tengo en mi tristeza una alegría...
sé que aún me quedan lágrimas.

61 (LXVIII)

I don't know what I dreamed
On the night past.
Sad, but sad, it must have been
For awake, the anguish lasts.

I noticed that the pillow
Was damp when I arose,
And for the first time, I was pleased
A bitter gladness filled my soul.

It's a sad thing, a dream
That leaves our eyes wet,
But in my sadness, I have one joy . . .
I know that I have tears left.

Espíritu sin nombre,
indefinible esencia,
yo vivo con la vida
sin formas de la idea.

Yo nado en el vacío,
del sol tiemblo en la hoguera,
palpito entre las sombras
y floto con las nieblas.

Yo soy el fleco de oro
de la lejana estrella,
yo soy de la alta luna
la luz tibia y serena.

Yo soy la ardiente nube
que en el ocaso ondea,
yo soy del astro errante
la luminosa estela.

Yo soy nieve en las cumbres,
soy fuego en las arenas,
azul onda en los mares,
y espuma en las riberas.

En el laúd soy nota,
perfume en la violeta,
fugaz llama en las tumbas
y en las ruinas yedra.

Yo atrueno en el torrente
y silbo en la centella,
y ciego en el relámpago
y rujo en la tormenta.

Yo río en los alcores,
susurro en la alta yerba,
suspiro en la onda pura
y lloro en la hoja seca.

Yo ondulo con los átomos
del humo que se eleva
y al cielo lento sube
en espiral inmensa.

Yo en los dorados hilos
que los insectos cuelgan

me mezco entre los árboles
en la ardorosa siesta.

Yo corro tras las ninfas
que en la corriente fresca
del cristalino arroyo
desnudas juguetean.

Yo, en bosques de corales
que alfombran blancas perlas,
persigo en el océano
las náyades ligeras.

Yo en las cavernas cóncavas
do el sol nunca penetra,
mezclándome a los gnomos
contemplo sus riquezas.

Yo busco de los siglos
las ya borradas huellas,
y sé de esos imperios
de que ni el nombre queda.

Yo sigo en raudo vértigo
los mundos que voltean,
y mi pupila abarca
la creación entera.

Yo sé de esas regiones
a do un rumor no llega,
y donde informes astros
de vida un soplo esperan.

Yo soy sobre el abismo
el puente que atraviesa,
yo soy la ignota escala
que el cielo une a la tierra,

Yo soy el invisible
anillo que sujeta
el mundo de la forma
al mundo de la idea.

Yo en fin soy ese espíritu,
desconocida esencia,
perfume misterioso
de que es vaso el poeta.

62 (V)

Nameless spirit
Ineffable essence,
I live a life
Of ideas without presence.

I swim in emptiness,
I flicker in the sun's blaze
I palpitate midst the shadows
And with the clouds I graze.

I am a distant star's
Golden sheen;
I am the light of the tall moon
Cool and serene.

I am, at end of day,
A rippling cloud burning;
In the wake of a meteor,
I am a gaseous churning.

I am snow on mountain tops,
I am fire in the sands,
A blue wave in the seas
And white foam on the strands.

I am the perfume of a violet,
I am the note of a lute,
In tombs, a fleeting flame,
And ivy in ruins mute.

I thunder in the torrents,
I hiss in lightning's flash,
I am the blinding light
And the tempest's crash.

I laugh in hills on high,
Waves carry the sighs I heave,
I murmur in the tall grass
And cry on dry leaves.

I vibrate with the atoms
Of smoke that rise,
Dancing in immense spirals
As it climbs to the skies.

I, on golden threads,
Woven on insects' looms,
Between the trees I sway
On sultry afternoons.

I chase after nymphs
In currents fresh,
Who, in crystaline brooks,
Gambol undressed.

I, in coral forests
Carpeted pearl white,
Pursue in the ocean
The naiads light.

I, in concave caverns
Where the sun never unfolds,
Mingling with gnomes,
Their riches I behold.

I look for the vanished traces
Of centuries lost in time,
I know the forgotten names
Of empires once sublime.

I follow in swift vertigo
The worlds in their gyrations,
And my eyes take in
All of creation.

I know of those regions
Unreached by sound and strife,
Where unformed stars
Silently await a breath of life.

I am the bridge by which
A chasm is spanned,
I am the unseen ladder
Which joins the heavens to land.

I am the invisible bond
Fashioned to bind
The world of form
To the world of the mind

I am, alas, that spirit
Unknown and irrefutable,
That mysterious elixir
For which the poet is the crucible.

141

Despierta, tiemblo al mirarte:
dormida, me atrevo a verte;
por eso, alma de mi alma,
yo velo mientras tú duermes.

Despierta ríes y al reir tus labios
inquietos me parecen
relámpagos de grana que serpean
sobre un cielo de nieve.

Dormida, los extremos de tu boca
pliega sonrisa leve,
suave como el rastro luminoso
que deja un sol que muere;
                    Duerme!

Despierta miras y al mirar tus ojos
húmedos resplandecen,
como la onda azul en cuya cresta
chispeando el sol hiere.

Al través de tus párpados, dormida;
tranquilo fulgor vierten
cual derrama de luz templado rayo
lámpara transparente.
                    Duerme!

Despierta hablas, y al hablar vibrantes
tus palabras parecen
lluvia de perlas que en dorada copa
se derrama a torrentes.

Dormida, en el murmullo de tu aliento
acompasado y tenue,
escucho yo un poema que mi alma
enamorada entiende.
                    Duerme!

Sobre el corazón la mano
me he puesto porque no suene
su latido y de la noche
turbe la calma solemne:

De tu balcón las persianas
cerré ya porque no entre
el resplandor enojoso
de la aurora y te despierte.
                    Duerme!

63 (XXVII)

Awake, I tremble when I look at you,
I dare to see you when your eyes close;
That's why, my dearest one,
I stay awake while you doze.

Awake, you laugh and then
Your restless lips glow
Like jagged streaks of scarlet
Lightning on a sky of snow.

Asleep, the corners of your mouth,
Fold into a smile ever so slight,
Soft like the tinted aura
Of they dying sun's fading light.

Sleep, my beloved!

Awake, your eyes dampened
By teardrops shine,
And like the sun,
On the crest of a wave, blind.

Through your closed eyelids
A gentle splendor glows,
Much like the soft light which
From a transparent lamp flows.

Sleep, my beloved!

Awake you speak, and on speaking,
Your vibrant words unfold
Like a rain of pearls spilled
In a torrent into a goblet of gold.

Asleep, in the rhythmic and thin
Murmur of your breath,
I listen to a poem which my loving soul
Understands in depth.

Sleep, my beloved!

Over my heart, I've put my hand
So that its beat may not be heard,
And so the solemn calm of night
May not be disturbed.

I've closed the blinds of your balcony
So that you do not wake
When in the angry splendor of dawn,
Daylight will break.

Sleep!

143

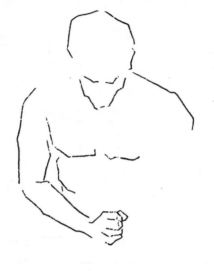

LXIV   (64)

Como guarda el avaro su tesoro,
guardaba mi dolor;
le quería probar que hay algo eterno
a la que eterno me juró su amor.

Mas hoy le llamo en vano y oigo al tiempo
que le agotó, decir:
¡Ah barro miserable! eternamente
no podrás ni aun sufrir!

64 (LXIV)

Like a miser hoards his treasure,
My suffering did I store,
I wanted to prove that there is something eternal
To the one who eternal love once swore.

But now I call upon it in vain, and I hear
Time, which exhausted it, say,
"Even your suffering will not be forever,
You worthless mass of clay!"

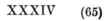

XXXIV (65)

Cruza callada, y son sus movimientos
silenciosa armonía:
suenan sus pasos; y al sonar recuerdan
del himno alado la cadencia rítmica.

Los ojos entreabre, aquellos ojos
tan claros como el día,
y la tierra y el cielo, cuanto abarcan
arden con nueva luz en sus pupilas.

Ríe, y su carcajada tiene notas
del agua fugitiva:
llora, y es cada lágrima un poema
de ternura infinita.

Ella tiene la luz, tiene el perfume,
el color y la línea,
la forma, engendradora de deseos,
la expresión, fuente eterna de poesía.

Que es estúpida? bah! mientras callando
guarde oscuro el enigma,
siempre valdrá lo que yo creo que calla
más que lo que cualquiera otra me diga.

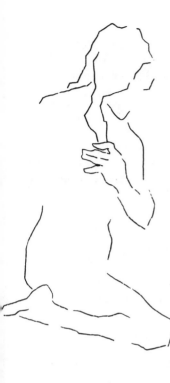

65 (XXXIV)

Silently she passes and her movements
Are mute harmony;
Her footsteps resound and call to mind
The rhythmic cadence of psalmody.

Her eyes she half opens,
Those eyes clear as sunlit skies,
And heaven and earth and all they embrace
Glow with new light in her eyes.

She laughs and her laughter carries
Notes of water rippling;
She cries, and each tear is a poem
Of tenderness infinite.

She has the light, the fragrance,
The color, form, and line,
That engender desire and inspiration,
Her expression, an eternal source of rhyme.

She is dull, you say? Bah!
As long as in silence she keeps a mystery,
What she leaves unsaid is worth more to me
Than what any other may say glibly.

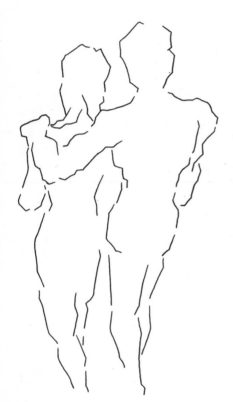

Su mano entre mis manos,
sus ojos en mis ojos,
la amorosa cabeza
apoyada en mi hombro,
Dios sabe cuántas veces
con paso perezoso
hemos vagado juntos
bajo los altos olmos
que de su casa prestan
misterio y sombra al pórtico.
Y ayer... un año apenas,
pasado como un soplo,
¡con qué exquisita gracia,
con qué admirable aplomo,
me dijo al presentarnos
un amigo oficioso:
«Creo que en alguna parte
he visto a usted.» ¡Ah bobos
que sois de los salones
comadres de buen tono
y andábais allí a caza
de galantes embrollos;
qué historia habéis perdido,
qué manjar tan sabroso
para ser devorado
sotto voce en un corro
detrás del abanico
de plumas y de oro!...

. . . .

¡Discreta y casta luna,
copudos y altos olmos,
paredes de su casa,
umbrales de su pórtico,
callad, y que el secreto
no salga de vosotros,
callad; que por mi parte
yo lo he olvidado todo:
y ella... ella, no hay máscara
semejante a su rostro.

66 (XL)

Her hand in my hands,
Her eyes on mine,
Her amorous head
Resting on my shoulder,
Lord know, how many times
We've wandered together,
Our steps lingering
Under the tall elms
Which to her house lend
Shadows and mystery.

And yesterday . . .
Scarcely a year,
Past like a breeze,
With such exquisite grace
With such admirable aplomb,
An officious friend
Told me on introducing us.
"I think that somewhere
I've seen you before.'
Oh, fools that you are,
You who frequent salons,
Fashionable midwives,
Searching in them
For amorous intrigues,
What a tale you've missed,
What a tasty morsel
To be devoured 'sotto voce'
In choral undertones,
Behind a fan
Of feathers and gold!

. . . .
Moon, discreet and chaste,
Tall and thicktopped elms,
Walls of her house,
Threshold of her door,
Be still; let the secret
Remain within you, safe,
Be still; for as for me,
I have forgotten all:
And as for her . . . her,
There is no mask
Like her face.

149

De dónde vengo? El más horrible y áspero
de los senderos busca;
las huellas de unos pies ensangrentados
sobre la roca dura;
los despojos de un alma hecha jirones
en las zarzas agudas,
te dirán el camino
que conduce a mi cuna.

Adónde voy? El más sombrío y triste
de los páramos cruza,
valle de eternas nieves y de eternas
melancólicas brumas.
En donde esté una piedra solitaria
sin inscripción alguna,
donde habite el olvido,
allí estará mi tumba.

67 (LXVI)

Where do I come from? Look
For the most horrible and rugged path;
For the traces of bloody feet
On the sharpest crags;
The shreds of a soul
In tatters, on brambles torn,
Will tell you the road
To where I was born.

Where am I going?
Cross the cold and somber waste,
The valley of eternal snows
And melancholy haze;
Where stands a solitary stone
Without even a name,
In oblivions' abode,
There you'll find my grave.

Como enjambre de abejas irritadas,
de un oscuro rincón de la memoria
salen a perseguirme los recuerdos
de las pasadas horas.

Yo los quiero ahuyentar. ¡Esfuerzo inútil!
Me rodean, me acosan,
y unos tras otros a clavarme vienen
el agudo aguijón que el alma encona.

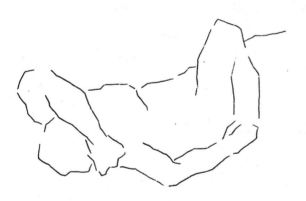

68 (LXIII)

Like a swarm of irritated bees,
Rushing from a dark corner of the mind,
There come to hound me, memories
Of other times.

I struggle to chase them, but alas,
They surround me and take their toll,
Wave on wave they come to pass
Stinging and infecting the soul.

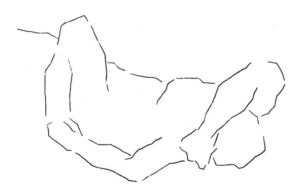

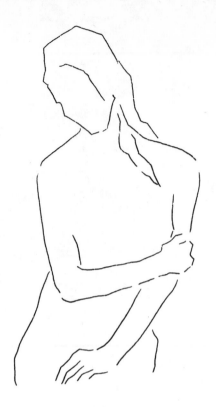

XXXIII   (69)

Es cuestión de palabras, y no obstante
ni tú ni yo jamás
después de lo pasado convendremos
en quién la culpa está.

¡Lástima que el Amor un diccionario
no tenga donde hallar
cuándo el orgullo es simplemente orgullo
y cuándo es dignidad!

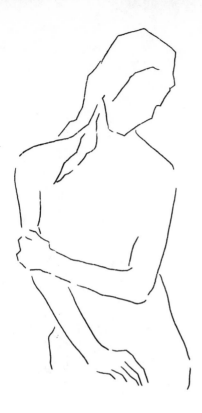

69 (XXXIII)

It's a matter of a word, yet all the same,
Neither you nor I will ever decide
Or agree, since our love has died,
Who should bear the blame.

Love has no dictionary; it's a shame,
There's no place to look inside
And see when pride is simply pride
Or when dignity is the proper name.

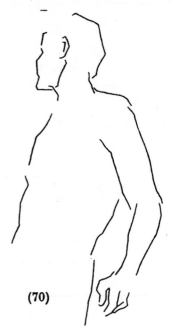

LI   (70)

De lo poco de vida que me resta
diera con gusto los mejores años,
por saber lo que a otros
de mí has hablado.

Y esta vida mortal y de la eterna
lo que me toque, si me toca algo,
por saber lo que a solas
de mí has pensado.

70 (LI)

Of the little of my life that's left,
I'd give with pleasure my best years,
If I could only hear
What to others of me you've said.

And this mortal life —— and of the unknown,
Whatever I'm granted if such there be,
To know what you've thought of me
When you were alone.

Cerraron sus ojos
que aún tenía abiertos,
taparon su cara
con un blanco lienzo,
y unos sollozando,
otros en silencio,
de la triste alcoba
todos se salieron.

La luz que en un vaso
ardía en el suelo
al muro arrojaba
la sombra del lecho
y entre aquella sombra
veíase a intérvalos
dibujarse rígida
la forma del cuerpo.

Despertaba el día,
y a su albor primero
con sus mil rüidos
despertaba el pueblo.
Ante aquel contraste
de vida y misterio,
de luz y tinieblas,
yo pensé un momento:

¡Dios mío, qué solos
se quedan los muertos!!

De la casa en hombros
lleváronla al templo
y en una capilla
dejaron el féretro.
Allí rodearon
sus pálidos restos
de amarillas velas
y de paños negros.

Al dar de las Ánimas
el toque postrero,
acabó una vieja
sus últimos rezos,
cruzó la ancha nave,
las puertas gimieron,
y el santo recinto
quedóse desierto.

De un reloj se oía
compasado el péndulo
y de algunos cirios
el chisporroteo.
Tan medroso y triste,
tan oscuro y yerto
todo se encontraba
que pensé un momento:

¡Dios mío, qué solos
se quedan los muertos!!

71 (LXXIII)

They closed her eyes
Which were yet unfastened,
With white linen,
Her face they matted;
And some sobbing,
Others in silence saddened,
The grief filled room
They all abandoned.

The candle burning
In a glass on the floor
Cast the shadow
Of her bed on the wall,
And in that faint glimmer,
From time to time, one saw
The rigid silhouette
Of the body's form.

At first light
The day was breaking,
And with its thousand noises,
The town was waking.
Before that contrast
Of life and the mystery awaiting,
Of light and darkness,
For a moment, I meditated:

The dead, my God,
How they remain forsaken!

From the house
They took the casket
To the church, on their shoulders,
And set it in the chapel.
Around her pallid remains
They dutifully added
Black drapery
And yellow candles.

At the stroke of Vespers'
Final tone,
Her prayers ended,
An old crone
Crossed the nave;
The doors groaned
And the holy place
Was left alone.

One could hear the pendulum
Of a clock swaying
And some long wax tapers'
Sparks spraying.
So fearsome and sad,
So dark and inanimated
Did everything seem
That for a moment, I meditated:

The dead, my God,
How they remain forsaken!

(continued)

De la alta campana
la lengua de hierro
le dio volteando
su adiós lastimero.
El luto en las ropas,
amigos y deudos
cruzaron en fila
formando el cortejo.

Del último asilo,
oscuro y estrecho,
abrió la piqueta
el nicho a un extremo:
allí la acostaron,
tapiáronle luego
y con un saludo
despidióse el duelo.

La piqueta al hombro
el sepulturero
cantando entre dientes
se perdió a lo lejos.
La noche se entraba,
el sol se había puesto:
perdido en las sombras
yo pensé un momento:

¡Dios mío, qué solos
se quedan los muertos!!

En las largas noches
del helado invierno,
cuando las maderas
crujir hace el viento
y azota los vidrios
el fuerte aguacero,
de la pobre niña
a veces me acuerdo.

Allí cae la lluvia
con un son eterno:
allí la combate
el soplo del cierzo.
Del húmedo muro
tendida en el hueco,
acaso de frío
se hielan sus huesos!...

. . . .

¿Vuelve el polvo al polvo?.
¿Vuela el alma al cielo?
¿Todo es sin espíritu [1]
podredumbre y cieno?
No sé; pero hay algo
que explicar no puedo,
algo que repugna [2]
aunque es fuerza hacerlo,
a dejar tan tristes
tan solos los muertos!

variantes

[1] ¿Todo es *vil materia.*

[2] *Que al par nos infunde*
repugnancia y duelo

160

71(cont'd)

The tongue of steel
Of the steeple bell
Ringing gave her
Its last farewell.
Dressed in mourning clothes,
Relatives and friends
Crossed in a row
Forming the cortege.

For her last abode.
Narrow and dark,
The pickaxe opened
A niche at one part:
There they laid her
And walled in the spot,
Then the mourners
Bid good—bye with a nod.

With pickaxe on his shoulder,
The gravedigger jaded,
Singing between his teeth,
Melted in the distant hazes.
Night was rising,
The sun had faded,
Lost in the shadows,
For a moment, I meditated:

The dead, my God,
How they remain foresaken!

On long nights
Of cold December,
When the wind makes
The timbers tremble,
And on the window, the downpour
Seems to last forever,
That poor girl,
I sometimes remember;

There falls the rain
With its eternal drone;
There beating upon her
The north wind blows.
In her niche in the wall
Humid and cold,
Perhaps the frost
Freezes her bones! . . .
. . . .
Does dust return to dust?
Does the soul rise to heaven in flight?
Is all vile matter,
Putrescence and slime?
I do not know, but there is
Something I cannot define,
Which evokes repugnance
And sorrow at the same time
On leaving so sad, so alone
Those who have died!

Te vi un punto, y flotando ante mis ojos
la imagen de tus ojos se quedó,
como la mancha oscura orlada en fuego
que flota y ciega si se mira al sol.

Adonde quiera que la vista clavo
torno a ver sus pupilas llamear
mas no te encuentro a tí; que es tu mirada,
unos ojos, los tuyos; nada más.

De mi alcoba en el ángulo los miro
desasidos fantásticos lucir:
cuando duermo los siento que se ciernen
de par en par abiertos sobre mí.

Yo sé que hay fuegos fatuos que en la noche
llevan al caminante a perecer:
yo me siento arrastrado por tus ojos,
pero a donde me arrastran no lo sé.

I saw you for a moment and, floating before my eyes,
The image of your eyes remained
Like the blinding sun girded with fire
Is seen darkly stained.

Wherever I choose to look,
I see those burning pupils of yours,
But I do not find you; what is your glance?
Eyes, your eyes, nothing more.

I see them in the corner of my room,
Eerily disembodied shine:
When I sleep, I feel them over me
Soaring, open wide.

I know that there are fatuous flames
That lead the wanderer till he dies;
I feel drawn, but I know not where,
Drawn relentlessly by your eyes.

Pasaba arrolladora en su hermosura
y el paso le dejé,
ni aun a mirarla me volví, y no obstante
algo a mi oído murmuró «ésa es».

¿Quién reunió la tarde a la mañana?
Lo ignoro: sólo sé
que en una breve noche de verano
se unieron los crepúsculos y «fue».

73 (XXXII)

She passed triumphant in her beauty,
And I stepped aside to let her go;
I didn't even give her a second glance, but
"She's the one," something in me whispered low.

Who was it that joined morning to the afternoon?
I can't say, but this I know,
That on a short summer night
Dawn and dusk were one, I saw her come and go.

En la imponente nave
del templo bizantino,
vi la gótica tumba a la indecisa
luz que temblaba en los pintados vidrios.

Las manos sobre el pecho,
y en las manos un libro,
una mujer hermosa reposaba
sobre la urna del cincel prodigio.

Del cuerpo abandonado
al dulce peso hundido,
cual si de blanda pluma y raso fuera
se plegaba su lecho de granito.

De la sonrisa última
el resplandor divino
guardaba el rostro, como el cielo guarda
del sol que muere el rayo fugitivo.

Del cabezal de piedra
sentados en el filo,
dos ángeles, el dedo sobre el labio,
imponían silencio en el recinto.

No parecía muerta;
de los arcos macizos
parecía dormir en la penumbra
y que en sueños veía el paraíso.

Me acerqué de la nave
al ángulo sombrío
con el callado paso que llegamos
junto a la cuna donde duerme un niño.

La contemplé un momento,
y aquel resplandor tibio,
aquel lecho de piedra que ofrecía
próximo al muro otro lugar vacío,

En el alma avivaron
la sed de lo infinito,
el ansia de esa vida de la muerte
para la que un instante son los siglos...

Cansado del combate
en que luchando vivo,
alguna vez me acuerdo con envidia
de aquel rincón oscuro y escondido.

De aquella muda y pálida
mujer me acuerdo y digo:
¡Oh, qué amor tan callado, el de la muerte!
¡Qué sueño el del sepulcro, tan tranquilo!

74 (LXXVI)

In the imposing nave
Of the Byzantine temple,
I saw the Gothic tomb in the vague
Light which on the stained glass trembled.

The hands over the bosom placed,
And in the hands, a tome,
Thus a beautiful woman graced
A sculptured casket's dome.

The abandoned body's weight,
As if it lay on satin,
Pressed upon and caused to plait
Her bed of solid granite.

Of her last smile remained
A heavenly splendor
Which her countenance retained
Like the sky, the dying sun's embers.

From the stone pillowcase,
Each on a corner seated,
Two angels, silence o'er the place,
With fingers on their lips entreated.

From the arches massive maze,
She did not appear deceased;
But as one sleeping in the shade,
Who dreaming glimpses heaven's peace.

I approached from the nave
To the niche's somber depths
As one comes upon a sleeping babe's
Cradle, with muffled steps.

I paused for a moment to ponder;
And that muted splendor which shone
Revealing an empty coffer
Next to that bed of stone

Awakened in my soul
A thirst for the infinite,
A longing for that life unknown
Where centuries are but a minute . .
. . . .
. . . .

Bored and tired of this state
In which I live, in struggle pitted,
Sometimes with envy, I relate
To that corner dark and hidden.

I remember that woman pale
And silent in that somber room.
Oh, what a quiet love that of the grave!
How peaceful the sleep of the tomb!

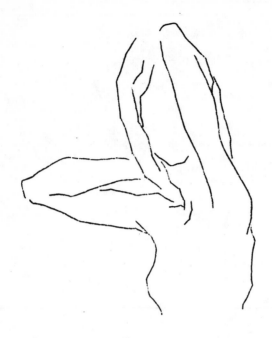

XXXIX (75)

A qué me lo decís? Lo sé: es mudable,
es altanera y vana y caprichosa:
antes que el sentimiento de su alma,
brotará el agua de la estéril roca.

Sé que en su corazón, nido de sierpes,
no hay una fibra que al amor responda;
que es una estatua inanimada... pero...
     ¡es tan hermosa!!

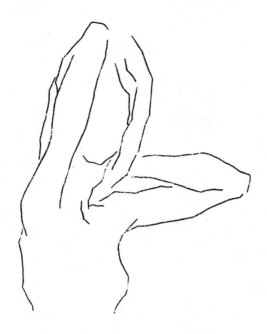

75 (XXXIX)

What is your purpose in telling me? I know:
She is flighty, and stubborn, haughty and vain;
Before any sentiment from her heart would flow,
Water from sterile rocks would drain.

I know that in her heart, a serpent's nest,
There isn't a fiber to respond to love;
She is an inanimate statue . . . but . . .
          She's so beautiful!

No dormía; vagaba en ese limbo
en que cambian de forma los objetos,
misteriosos espacios que separan
la vigilia del sueño.

Las ideas que en ronda silenciosa
daban vueltas en torno a mi cerebro,
poco a poco en su danza se movían
con un compás más lento.

De la luz que entra al alma por los ojos
los párpados velaban el reflejo;
mas otra luz el mundo de visiones
alumbraba por dentro.

En este punto resonó en mi oído
un rumor semejante al que en el templo
vaga confuso al terminar los fieles
con un *Amén* sus rezos.

Y oí como una voz delgada y triste
que por mi nombre me llamó a lo lejos,
y sentí olor de cirios apagados
de humedad y de incienso!

. . . .
. . . .

Entró la noche y del olvido en brazos
caí cual piedra en su profundo seno:
Dormí y al despertar exclamé: «Alguno
que yo quería ha muerto!»

I couldn't sleep. I wandered in that limbo
In which the forms of objects change,
In that mysterious space separating
Sleep from a wakeful state.

The ideas which in a silent round
Spun back and forth within my head
Began dancing little by little
In a more restful step.

My eyelids stood guard against the glare
Which enters the soul through the eyes,
But the inner world of visions
Lit another light inside.

At that   moment, there echoed in my ear,
A rumbling like the one that fills the air
Of a temple when the faithful,
With an 'Amen' end their prayer.

I heard my name being called
By a voice thin and remote,
And I smelled the odor
Of incense and candle smoke.

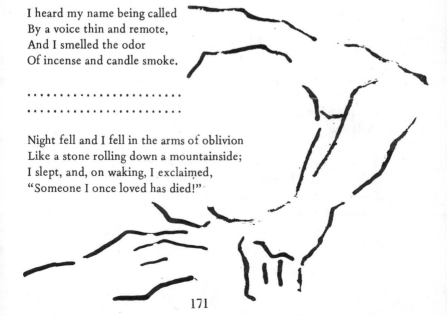

. . . .
. . . .

Night fell and I fell in the arms of oblivion
Like a stone rolling down a mountainside;
I slept, and, on waking, I exclaimed,
"Someone I once loved has died!"

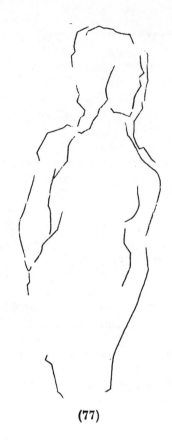

XLVI (77)

Me ha herido recatándose en las sombras,
sellando con un beso su traición.
Los brazos me echó al cuello y por la espalda
partióme a sangre fría el corazón.

Y ella prosigue alegre su camino
feliz, risueña, impávida ¿y por qué?
Porque no brota sangre de la herida,
porque el muerto está en pie.

77 (XLVI)

She wounded me and hid in the shadows;
Her arms around my neck,
She sealed her treason with a kiss;
In cold blood, my heart was rent.

And she merrily goes about,
Radiant, calm, and content;
Because no blood flows from the wound,
The dead man is not yet dead.

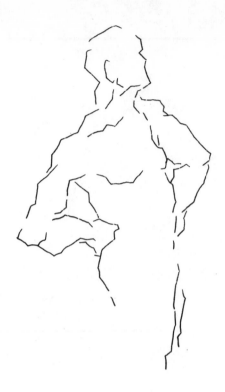

XXXV

No me admiró tu olvido! Aunque de un día,
me admiró tu cariño mucho más;
porque lo que hay en mí que vale algo
eso... ni lo pudiste sospechar.

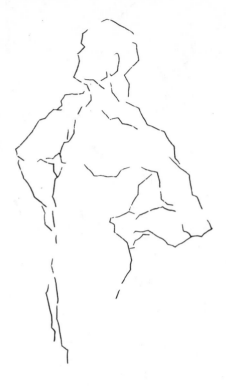

78 (XXXV)

I do not wonder that you've forgotten me!
Once, I was even more surprised by your caress;
For what there is in me of worth . . .
That . . . you couldn't even guess!

Porque son niña tus ojos
verdes como el mar, te quejas;
verdes los tienen las náyades,
verdes los tuvo Minerva,
y verdes son las pupilas
de las hurís del Profeta.

El verde es gala y ornato
del bosque en la primavera,
entre sus siete colores
brillante el Iris lo ostenta,
las esmeraldas son verdes,
verde el color del que espera
y las ondas del océano
y el laurel de los poetas.

Es tu mejilla, temprana
rosa de escarcha cubierta
en que el carmín de los pétalos
se ve al través de las perlas.
        Y sin embargo
        sé que te quejas
        porque tus ojos
        crees que la afean:
        pues no lo creas.
Que parecen sus pupilas
húmedas verdes e inquietas
tempranas hojas de almendro
que al soplo del aire tiemblan.

Es tu boca de rubíes
purpúrea granada abierta
que en el estío convida
a apagar la sed con ella.
        Y sin embargo
        sé que te quejas
        porque tus ojos
        crees que la afean:
        pues no lo creas.
Que parecen si enojada
tus pupilas centellean
las olas del mar que rompen
en las cantábricas peñas.

Es tu frente que corona
crespo el oro en ancha trenza
nevada cumbre en que el día
su postrera luz refleja.
        Y sin embargo
        sé que te quejas
        porque tus ojos
        crees que la afean:
        pues no lo creas.
Que entre las rubias pestañas
junto a las sienes semejan
broches de esmeralda y oro
que un blanco armiño sujetan.

Porque son niña tus ojos
verdes como el mar te quejas,
quizá si negros o azules
se tornasen lo sintieras.

Dear one, do you complain
Because your eyes are green;
Green were Minerva's eyes,
Green the eyes of the undines,
And green are the pupils
Of the houris of Mohammed's dreams.

Green is the garment and the halo
Of a forest in the spring,
The seven colored rainbow
Is proudest of its green,
Green is the color of emeralds,
The color an ocean wave heaves,
The color of he who waits,
And of the poets' laurel wreaths.

An early rose covered
With frost is your cheek;
Through its pearls, the petals'
Crimson hue is seen.
    And nevetheless,
      You complain, I perceive,
      Your eyes make you
      Plain, you believe:
    Well, be at ease.
For one can see in your eyes
Restless, damp, and green,
The trembling in the wind
Of early leaves on almond trees.

You mouth is of rubies,
A pomegranate baring its meat
Which invites one to quench
One's thirst midst summer's heat.
    And nevetheless,
      You complain, I perceive,
      Your eyes make you
      Plain, you believe:
    Well, be at ease.
For your eyes sparkle,
If angry you seem,
Like waves which break
On Cantabrian peaks.

Your forehead crowned
By wide tresses in golden rings,
Is a snowy summit which reflects
The dying day's light and heat.
    And nevertheless,
      You complain, I perceive,
      Your eyes make you
      Plain, you believe:
    Well, be at ease.
For your blond lashes
Together with your temples seem
Like brooches of emerald and gold
Holding white ermine in between.

Because your eyes are green
As the sea, do you complain my dear;
If black or blue they were to be
Tomorrow, you might then also grieve.

LXXX

Es un sueño la vida,
pero un sueño febril que dura un punto;
cuando de él se despierta,
se ve que todo es vanidad y humo...

¡Ojalá fuera un sueño
muy largo y muy profundo,
un sueño que durara hasta la muerte!...
Yo soñaría con mi amor y el tuyo.

Life is a dream,
A feverish one that lasts for just a moment;
One can see that all is smoke and vanity
When the dream is over . . .

Oh, if it were only a dream
Very long and very profound,
A dream that would last until death! . . .
I would dream of this love we've found.

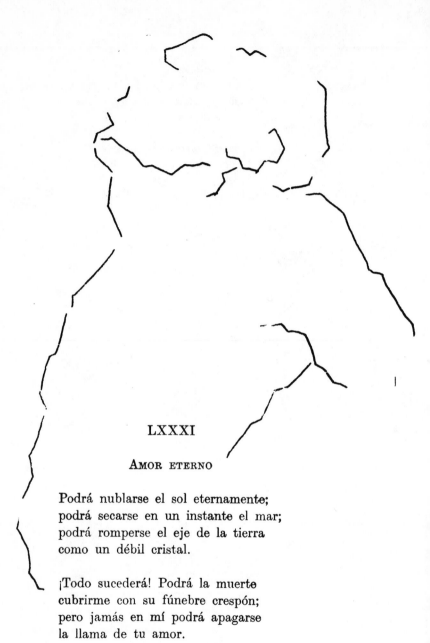

LXXXI

Amor eterno

Podrá nublarse el sol eternamente;
podrá secarse en un instante el mar;
podrá romperse el eje de la tierra
como un débil cristal.

¡Todo sucederá! Podrá la muerte
cubrirme con su fúnebre crespón;
pero jamás en mí podrá apagarse
la llama de tu amor.

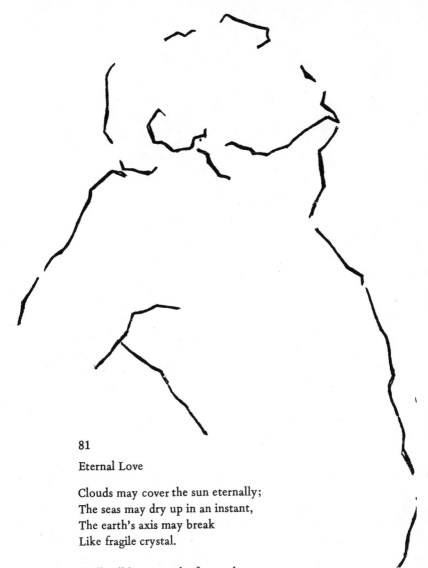

81

Eternal Love

Clouds may cover the sun eternally;
The seas may dry up in an instant,
The earth's axis may break
Like fragile crystal.

It all will happen, The funereal crepe
Of death may cover me from above;
But never will it extinguish in me
The flame of your love.

ERRANTE por el mundo fuí gritando:
  ¡La gloria dónde está?
Y una voz misteriosa contestóme:
  Más allá... más allá...
En pos de ella seguí por el camino
  que la voz me marcó,
halléla al fin, pero en aquel instante
  en humo se trocó.
Mas el humo, formando denso velo,
  se empezó a remontar:
y penetrando en la azulada esfera
  al cielo fué a parar.

82

I wandered through the world shouting:
"Glory, where can it be?"
——"Further on . . . Further on . . ."
A mysterious voice answered me.

In pursuit, I followed along the path
The voice indicated when it spoke.
I found it at last, but in that moment,
It changed into smoke.

Then the smoke, forming a dense veil,
Slowly began to rise,
And reaching the blue of heaven,
It lodged in the skies.

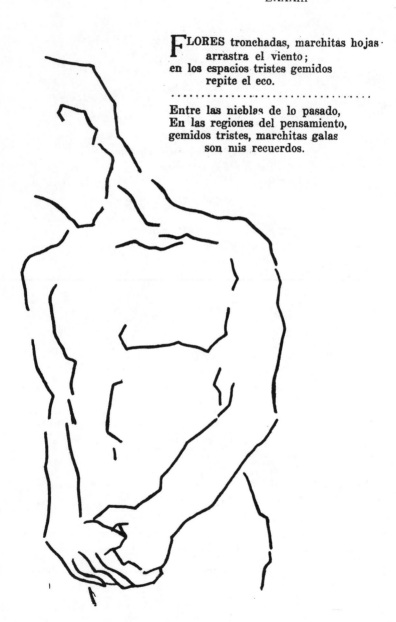

Flores tronchadas, marchitas hojas
    arrastra el viento;
en los espacios tristes gemidos
    repite el eco.

. . . .

Entre las nieblas de lo pasado,
En las regiones del pensamiento,
gemidos tristes, marchitas galas
    son mis recuerdos.

The wind blows cut flowers
And withered leaves;
Sorrowful moans in space,
The echo repeats.

. . . .

Midst the mist of the past,
In the regions of reverie,
Faded trappings, sorrowful moans
Remain in my memory.

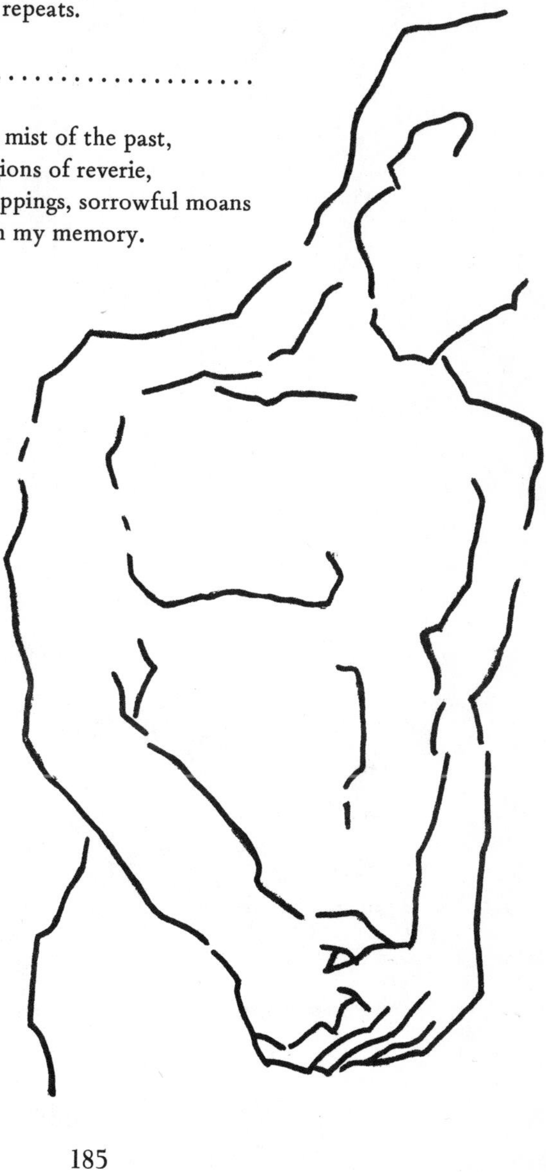

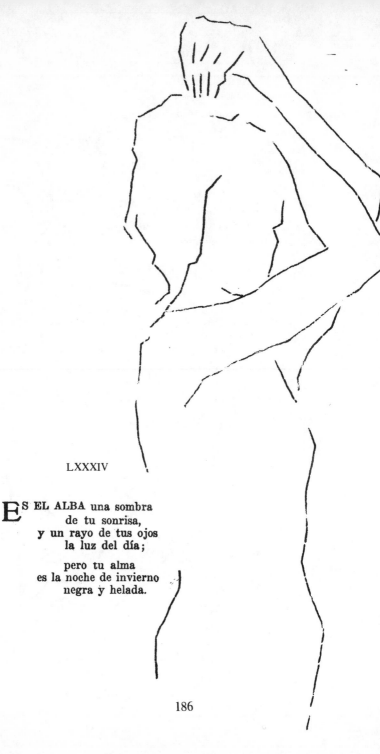

LXXXIV

Es EL ALBA una sombra
            de tu sonrisa,
    y un rayo de tus ojos
        la luz del día;

        pero tu alma
    es la noche de invierno
        negra y helada.

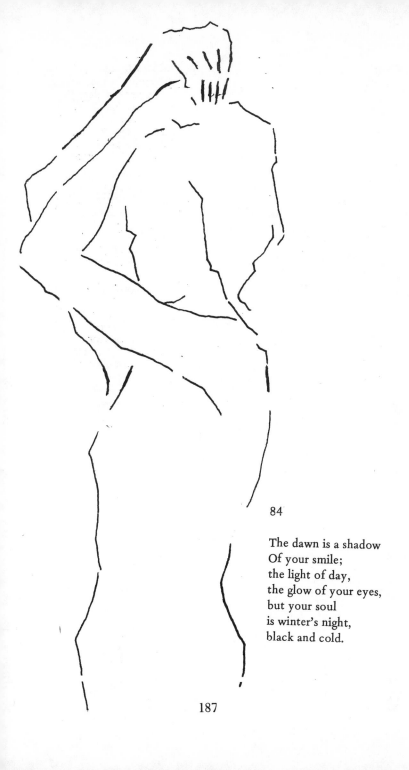

84

The dawn is a shadow
Of your smile;
the light of day,
the glow of your eyes,
but your soul
is winter's night,
black and cold.

NEGROS fantasmas,
    nubes sombrías,
huyen ante el destello
de luz divina.
Esa luz santa,
niña de ojos negros,
es la esperanza.

    Al calor de sus rayos
mi fe gigante,
contra desdenes lucha
sin amenguarse.

En este empeño
es, si grande el martirio,
mayor el premio.

    Y si aun muestras esquiva
alma de nieve,
si aun no me quisieras,
yo he de quererte.
Mi amor es roca
donde se estrellan tímidas
del mal las olas.

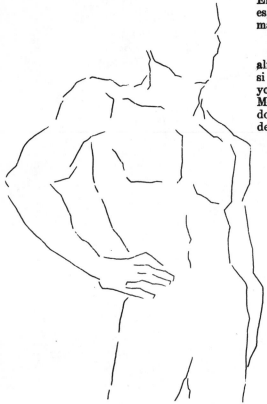

Black phantoms,
Clouds in somber flight,
Flee before the flashing
Of Holy Light.
        That saintly glow,
        Oh, dark eyed maiden
        Is naught, but hope.

At the heat of its rays,
My faith infinite
Fights against disdains
Without diminishing.
        If martyrdom be great
        In this engagement,
        Still greater is the gain,

And if you still be haughty
And show a soul of snow,
If still you do not love me,
Shall I not love you? No!
        My love is like a rock
        On which waves timidly
        Break of the shock.

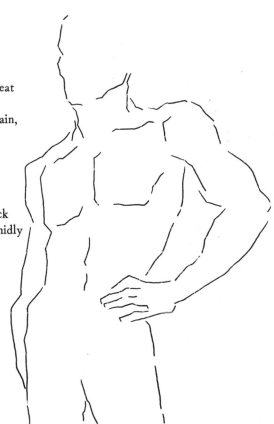

Yo soy el rayo, la dulce brisa;
lágrima ardiente, fresca sonrisa;
flor peregrina, rama tronchada;
    yo soy quien vibra,
    flecha acerada.

Hay en mi esencia, como en las flores,
de mil perfumes suaves vapores;
y su fragancia fascinadora
trastorna el alma de quien adora.

Yo mis aromas doquier prodigo,
y el más horrible dolor mitigo;
y en grato, dulce, tierno delirio,
cambio el más dulce, crüel martirio.
¡Ay!, yo encadeno los corazones,
mas son de flores mis eslabones.

Navego por los mares,
    voy por el viento;
alejo los pesares
    del pensamiento.
    Yo dicha o pena
reparto a los mortales
    con faz serena.

Poder terrible, que en mis antojos
brota sonrisas o brota enojos;
poder que abrasa un alma helada;
    si airado vibro,
    flecha acerada.

Doy las dulces sonrisas a las hermosas,
coloro sus mejillas de nieve y rosas;
humedezco sus labios, y a sus miradas
hago prometer dichas no imaginadas.
Yo hago amable el reposo, grato, halagüeño,
o alejo de los seres el dulce sueño.

Todo a mi poderío rinde homenaje,
todos a mi corona dan vasallaje;
soy amor, rey del mundo, niña tirana;
    ámame, y tú la reina
    serás mañana.

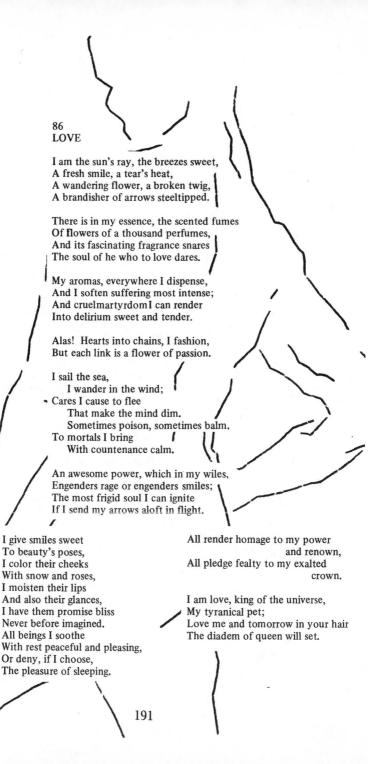

86
LOVE

I am the sun's ray, the breezes sweet,
A fresh smile, a tear's heat,
A wandering flower, a broken twig,
A brandisher of arrows steeltipped.

There is in my essence, the scented fumes
Of flowers of a thousand perfumes,
And its fascinating fragrance snares
The soul of he who to love dares.

My aromas, everywhere I dispense,
And I soften suffering most intense;
And cruel martyrdom I can render
Into delirium sweet and tender.

Alas! Hearts into chains, I fashion,
But each link is a flower of passion.

I sail the sea,
    I wander in the wind;
Cares I cause to flee
        That make the mind dim.
        Sometimes poison, sometimes balm,
To mortals I bring
        With countenance calm.

An awesome power, which in my wiles,
Engenders rage or engenders smiles;
The most frigid soul I can ignite
If I send my arrows aloft in flight.

I give smiles sweet
To beauty's poses,
I color their cheeks
With snow and roses,
I moisten their lips
And also their glances,
I have them promise bliss
Never before imagined.
All beings I soothe
With rest peaceful and pleasing,
Or deny, if I choose,
The pleasure of sleeping.

All render homage to my power
                    and renown,
All pledge fealty to my exalted
                    crown.

I am love, king of the universe,
My tyranical pet;
Love me and tomorrow in your hair
The diadem of queen will set.

191

LXXXVII

¿No HAS SENTIDO en la noche,
cuando reina la sombra,
una voz apagada que canta
y una inmensa tristeza que llora?

¿No sentiste en tu oído de virgen
las silentes y trágicas notas
que mis dedos de muerto arrancaban
a la lira rota?

¿No sentiste una lágrima mía
deslizarse en tu boca?
¿Ni sentiste mi mano de nieve
estrechar a la tuya de rosa?

¿No viste entre sueños
por el aire vagar una sombra,
ni sintieron tus labios un beso
que estalló misterioso en la alcoba?

Pues yo juro por ti, vida mía,
que te vi entre mis brazos, miedosa,
que sentí tu aliento de jazmín y nardo
y tu boca pegada a mi boca.

87

Have you not heard at night
When dark shadows reign,
A muffled voice which sings
And a sad cry of endless pain?

Did you not hear in your chaste ear
The silent and tragic strains
Which my deadman's fingertips
On a broken lyre played?

Haven't you felt one of my tears
Fall upon your lips below,
Nor feel in your rosy hand
My withered hand of snow?

Haven't you seen in your dreams
A shadow drifting through the air;
Didn't your lips feel a kiss
Mysterious which in your bedroom flared?

Well I swear on your life, my dear,
That I saw you shy in my arms one night;
I felt your breath of jasmine and nard,
And your mouth on mine pressed tight.

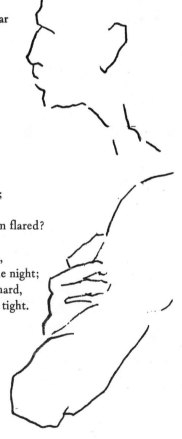

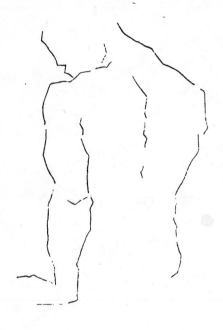

LXXXVIII

YO ME ACOGÍ, como perdido nauta,
   a una mujer para pedirla amor,
y fué su amor, cansancio a mis sentidos,
   hielo a mi corazón.

Y quedé de mi vida, en la carrera
que un mundo de esperanza ayer pobló,
como queda un viandante en el desierto:
   ¡a solas con su Dios!

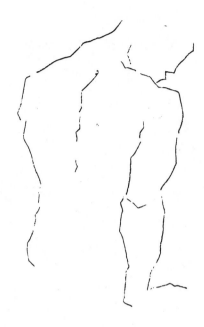

88

I clung like a shipwrecked sailor
To a woman, wooing her love with pleas,
And her love was boredom to my senses;
     It made my heart freeze.

And I remained, in the course of my life,
Where once a world of hope was stored,
Like a wanderer remains in the desert:
     Alone with his Lord!

LXXXIX

¡QUIÉN fuera luna,
   quién fuera brisa,
quién fuera sol!
. . . .

   ¡Quién del crepúsculo
fuera la hora,
quién el instante
de tu oración;
quién fuera parte
de la plegaria
que solitaria
mandas a Dios!
. . . .

   ¡Quién fuera luna,
quién fuera brisa,
quién fuera sol!...

89

Who could be the moonlight,
Who could be the breeze,
Who could   be the sunshine!

. . . .

Who could be
The hour of dawn,
Who, the motivation
Of your prayer sublime;

Who could be a part
Of the supplication
That in isolation,
You send to the Lord divine!

Who could be the moonlight,
Who could be the breeze,
Who could be the sunshine!

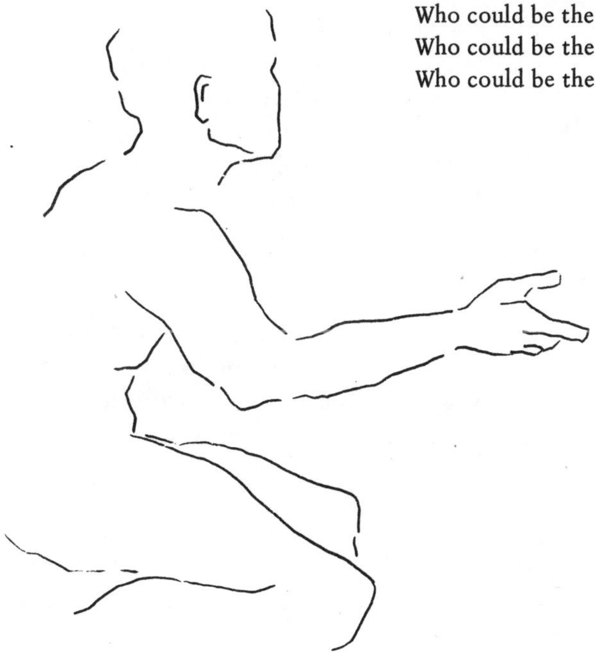

DE NOCHE

Apoyando mi frente calurosa
en el frío cristal de la ventana,
en el silencio de la oscura noche
de su balcón mis ojos no apartaba.

En medio de la sombra misteriosa
su vidriera lucía iluminada,
dejando que mi vista penetrase
en el puro santuario de su estancia.

Pálido como el mármol el semblante,
la blonda cabellera destrénzada,
acariciando sus sedosas ondas,
sus hombros de alabastro y su garganta,
mis ojos la veían, y mis ojos
al verla tan hermosa, se turbaban.

Mirábase al espejo; dulcemente
sonreía a su bella imagen lánguida,
y sus mudas lisonjas al espejo
con un beso dulcísimo pagaba...

Mas la luz se apagó; la visión pura
desvanecióse como sombra vana,
y dormido quedé, dándome celos
el cristal que su boca acariciara.

90

At Night

Resting my feverish forehead
On the cold windowpane,
In the silence of the dark night,
My eyes on her balcony I trained.

A light in her window shined
In the midst of the somber gloom,
Allowing my eyes to penetrate
The chaste sanctuary of her room.

Her face, pale as marble,
Her blond hair flowing free,
Its silken waves caressing
Her shoulders, I could see,
And on seeing her,
Her beauty blinded me.

She was looking at her mirror smiling
Sweetly at her image so langorous,
And to the mirror for its mute flattery,
She gave a kiss so amorous.

But the light went out; the vision
Like an empty shadow evanesced,
And I fell asleep, jealously envying
The glass on which her lips had pressed.

XCI

Si copia tu frente
del río cercano la pura corriente
y miras tu rostro de amor encendido,
 soy yo, que me escondo
 del agua en el fondo
y loco de amores a amar te convido;
soy yo, que en tu pecho buscando morada,
envío a tus ojos mi ardiente mirada,
 mi llama divina...
y el fuego que siento la faz te ilumina.

Si en medio del valle
en tardo se trueca tu andar animado,
vacila tu plantá, se pliega tu talle...
 soy yo, dueño amado,
 que en no vistos lazos
de amor anhelante, te estrecho en mis brazos;
soy yo, quien te teje la alfombra florida
que vuelve a tu cuerpo la fuerza y la vida;
 soy yo, que te sigo
en alas del viento soñando contigo.

Si estando en tu lecho
escuchas acaso celeste armonía
que llena de goces tu cándido pecho,
 soy yo, vida mía...
 soy yo, que levanto
al cielo tranquilo mi férvido canto;
soy yo, que los aires cruzando ligero
por un ignorado movible sendero,
 ansioso de calma,
sediento de amores, penetro en tu alma.

91

If your forehead is mirrored
In the crystal currents of the nearby river,
And you see your face with love alight,
　　　It is I, aglow,
　　　Hiding in the depths below
Who mad with love, to love I invite;
It is I, who, in your heart seeking a place,
Casts my ardent eyes on yours;
　　　My divine flame roars,
And the passion I feel casts light on your face.

If in the midst of a vale,
Your sprightly step is slowed,
Your body bends and your feet fail . . .
　　　It is I, with love bold,
　　　Who is unseen bonds
Of amorous desire, holds you in my arms;
It is I, who weaves for you the flowering weft
Which brings back to your body its life and strength;
　　　It is I, who following, dreams
Of you on the wind's invisible wings;

If while lying in your bed,
Celestial harmonies you hear,
Which fill with delight your candorous breast.
　　　It is I my dear . . .
　　　Raising to the tranquil sky
My ardent song; it is I,
Who through the air crossing fast
In an unseen and unknown path,
　　　Longing for calm,
Thirsting for love, penetrates your heart.

XCII

La gota de rocío

La gota de rocío que en el cáliz
duerme de la blanquísima azucena,
es el palacio de cristal en donde
vive el genio feliz de la pureza.
Él le da su misterio y poesía,
él su aroma balsámico le presta;
¡ay de la flor si de la luz al beso
se evapora esa perla!

92
The Dewdrop

The dewdrop which sleeps
In the calyx of the lily white,
Is the palace of crystal
Where dwells Purity's happy sprite.

He gives it its mystery and poetry,
He lends it balmy aromas at night,
Oh, pity the flower if this pearl
Evaporates at the kiss of light!

XCIII

A Casta

Tu aliento es el aliento de las flores;
tu voz es de los cisnes la armonía;
es tu mirada el esplendor del día,
y el color de la rosa es tu color.

Tú prestas nueva vida y esperanza
a un corazón para el amor ya muerto;
tú creces de mi vida en el desierto
como crece en el páramo la flor.

—

93

TO CASTA

Your breath is the fragrance of a flower;
Your voice, the harmony of swans;
Your glance is the day's splendorous calm,
And the color of the rose is your radiance.

In the desert of my life you tower;
New life and new hope you lend
To a heart for love already dead,
Like a flower growing in a wasteland.

XCIV

Lejos y entre los árboles
de la intrincada selva
¿no ves algo que brilla
y llora? Es una estrella.

Ya se la ve más próxima,
como a través de un tul,
de una ermita en el pórtico
brillar. Es una luz.

De la carrera rápida
el término está aquí.
Desilusión. No es lámpara ni estrella
la luz que hemos seguido: es un candil.

206

94

Distant and midst the trees
Of a jungle thick and far,
Don't you see something shine
And cry? It's a star.

Closer, as if through tulle,
You see it veiled in sight;
In the doorway of a hermitage,
Flickering. It's a light.

What disillusion awaits
At the end of the race rapid.
It isn't a light or a star
We've followed. It's a candle.

XCV

A Todos los Santos

(1.º de noviembre)

Patriarcas que fuisteis la semilla
del árbol de la fe en siglos remotos,
al vencedor divino de la muerte
rogadle por nosotros.

Profetas que rasgasteis inspirados
del porvenir el velo misterioso,
al que sacó la luz de las tinieblas
rogadle por nosotros.

Almas cándidas, Santos Inocentes
que aumentáis de los ángeles el coro,
al que llamó a los niños a su lado
rogadle por nosotros.

Apóstoles que echasteis en el mundo
de la Iglesia el cimiento poderoso,
al que es de la verdad depositario
rogadle por nosotros.

Mártires que ganasteis vuestra palma
en la arena del circo, en sangre rojo,
al que os dio fortaleza en los combates
rogadle por nosotros.

Vírgenes semejantes a azucenas,
que el verano vistió de nieve y oro,
al que es fuente de vida y hermosura
rogadle por nosotros.

Monjes que de la vida en el combate
pedisteis paz al claustro silencioso,
al que es iris de calma en las tormentas
rogadle por nosotros.

Doctores cuyas plumas nos legaron
de virtud y saber rico tesoro,
al que es raudal de ciencia inextinguible
rogadle por nosotros.

Soldados del ejército de Cristo,
Santas y Santos todos,
rogadle que perdone nuestras culpas
a Aquel que vive y reina entre vosotros.

95

TO ALL SAINTS
(November 1st)

Ye patriarchs who were the seed
Of the tree of faith in centuries before us,
To the divine conqueror of death,
Pray to Him for us.

Ye prophets who tore from the future
Its veil mysterious with inspired forces,
To the one who brought light out of darkness,
Pray to Him for us.

Ye pure souls, Holy Innocents
Who augment the angel's chorus,
To the one who called children to his side,
Pray to Him for us.

Ye Apostles who laid in this world
The foundation of the Church most glorious,
To the one who is depositary of truth,
Pray to Him for us.

Ye martyrs who won your palm
In the Coliseum's red and gory dust,
To the one who gave you strength in combat,
Pray to Him for us.

Ye virgins like unto white lilies
Which summer dressed in snow and golden rust,
To the one who is the fountain of life and beauty,
Pray to Him for us.

Ye monks who sought peace in silent cloisters
From the struggles of a life more boisterous,
To the one who is the rainbow of calm in tempests,
Pray to Him for us.

Ye theologians whose pen left a legacy,
Of virtue and knowledge a rich thesaurus,
To the one who is the source of eternal wisdom,
Pray to Him for us.

Soldiers in the army of Christ,
All ye saints that have been,
To the one who lives and reigns among you,
Pray that He pardon our sins.

TRANSLATOR'S

NOTE

TRANSLATOR'S NOTE

"Traduttore—traditore." A translator is a traitor they say in Italian, and so, let me confess my infidelity. I will not attempt to exonerate myself by claiming that it was necessary to change a word here and there or, in many cases, the word order for the sake of making the 'rimas' rhyme in English, though this is indeed true. The intent throughout this volume has been to convey the musicality and subtle charm of Becquer's verse. If I have succeeded to any extent in this endeavor, as I hope I have, then, in the end, I have been faithful to Becquer.

Becquer's Ars Poetica

In discussing Becquer's concept of poetry, one must refer to the memorable distinction he draws between the poetry of the mind and that of the heart, which appears in the prologue he wrote to a collection of popular Andalusian ballads by his friend, Augusto Ferran, entitled, La soledad.

"There is a magnificent and sonorous poetry; a poetry...adorned with all the pomp of the language, which moves in majestic cadences.

"There is another poetry, natural, short, and dry, which surges from the heart like a spark of electricity, which touches one's sentiments with a word and flees, and, devoid of artifice, unencumbered within a free form, it awakens a thousand ideas which sleep in the bottomless ocean of fantasy...

"The first is a melody which is born, develops, ends, and disappears.

"The second is a chord plucked from a harp, and the strings remain vibrating with a harmonious ring...

"One is the divine fruit of the union of art and imagination.

"The other is a flash of fire given off by the impact of sentiment and passion.

"The poems in this book [La soledad] belong to the latter of the two types, because they are popular, and popular poetry is the synthesis of poetry."

Symphony of Love is the title I have chosen for this translation of the Rimas, because Becquer is, above all, the poet of love. To Becquer, love is both the source of the creative process and the key to the eternal mystery; it is art; it is religion. The longing for death, and the anguish of creation found in his work are themes that orchestrate this central theme of love, blending with it or atonally contrasting it, extending it always to the totality of the poet's existence.

In the Cartas literarias a una mujer, a series of four essays which appeared in 1860, Becquer expounds this thought of the oneness of poetry and beauty, love and religion. The first letter begins with an echo of Rima 21 (XXI), which ends with the powerful declaration, "Poesía ... eres tú", alluding to a previous occasion on which his beloved had asked him what poetry was and he had answered after some hesitation, "Poetry...why it is you." The question was an attempt to penetrate that mysterious sanctuary in which Becquer's soul found refuge. His first intention then, is to assuage any doubts she may have had regarding the sincerity of his reply. Knowing that his answer may have seemed offhandish at the moment, perhaps a trifle too gallant, he reiterates the refrain, elaborating on its full meaning:

"Poetry is you, because that vague aspiration to what is beautiful, which characterizes it, and which in man is a faculty of the mind, may be said to be an instinct in you.

"Poetry is you, because sentiment, which is an accidental phenomenon in us ... is found so intimately joined to your particular make-up, that it constitutes a part of your very being...

"Poetry is in man a quality, purely of the spirit; it resides in his soul, it lives the intangible life of ideas, and in order to reveal it, he needs to give it form. It is for this reason that he writes it."

In the second and third letters, Becquer carries this thought further, beginning with the statement that "... poetry is you, because you are the most beautiful personification of sentiment,..." and extending it to speak of love, at the same time, equating love with religion.

"Yes, love is the perennial source of all poetry, the fertile origin of all that is great, the eternal beginning of all that is beautiful; and I say love, because religion, our religion, above all, is also a love..."

"...love is the supreme law of the universe ... God is the origin of those thousand unknown thoughts, which are all poetry...

"Poetry is nothing else, but that vague and melancholy aspiration which moves your heart with the desire for an impossible perfection."

It is in the fourth and last letter that he brings his definition of poetry to its full sublimation. It begins axiomatically, in the language of Euclidian geometry, "Love is poetry: religion is love. Two things equal to a third are equal to each other." Further on, he repeats, "Religion is love, and, because it is love, it is poetry." What follows is a tale of what he imagined on a day he spent sketching the statues in the convent of San Juan de los Reyes in Toledo. The sanctity and the antiquity of the cloister captivated his spirit. Hooded monks and haloed virgins seemed to move in the dusk of twilight; a generation in granite on whose faces shone an expression of beautitude and ineffable serenity. "Is it possible," he asked, "that you have lived without passions, without fear, without hope, nor desire? Who has gathered the emanations of love, which like an arome, issued from your souls?" It was then that he noticed that these emaciated figures had their eyes turned upward, peering into the infinite, looking for God. "God, the source, eternal and ardent of beauty, to whom we turn our eyes, like unto a lode-star of love, the sentiment of the soul."

To Becquer then, the source of inspiration is that deep emotion felt in the mystical transport of the soul in union with the divine essence, though its focus may be the sentiment of love for a woman, or the contemplation of beauty in any form. It is spiritual; it is sensual—the two are one. They are both the handiwork of the Creator, and the creative process in man is also divine in its source and in its manifestation.

What the poet feels is stored in his heart awaiting that moment when his mind finds the words needed to express it.

> "Everyone feels. It is only given to a few beings to hold like a treasure, the vivid memory of what they have felt. I believe that these are the poets. What's more, I believe that it is only because of this that they are poets."

This thought is echoed in the Introduccion sinfonica in which Becquer expresses his anxiety to cast off those visions that circulate within his brain: the confused names and dates of women and days that had passed or had never existed except in his mind—the extravagant children of his fantasy. They are, as he says, sensations that have left their mark upon him either because of their tangible reality or because of the intensity of the impression of what he has imagined. At a given moment, a glorious one for the poet, these feelings burst forth, his hand almost mechanically writing the dictates of his mind, in which these vague and confused sensations have grown to full maturity and now demand to be born.

But the poet must envelop them in a form! Elsewhere in the Cartas literarias a une mujer, he speaks of the need for order. "I detest it," he says, "but it is so necessary for everything." In Rima 42 (III), he describes the fervor of inspiration and then the cool stream of reason in which, "fever's thirst is abated,"—reason, whose imperious voice "orients the mind's chaos." The artist's debt to both reason and inspiration is expressed in the last stanza,

> "With both always in conflict,
> And master of them both,
> Only the genius can tie the two
> To one yoke."

Becquer's Life (Feb. 17, 1836 - Dec. 22, 1870)

There has arisen about Becquer a kind of mystique which romanticizes the tragedy and misery that pervaded much of his life. Indeed, it is difficult to separate Becquer, the man, from Becquer, the poet of the Rimas, for to do so is to isolate his soul from the events that occurred to the body in which it lodged for the brief span of thirty four years.

There are those who would see all that happened to him in terms of his writing, and create of him the image of romantic gloom and despair. But it is to be borne in mind that Art did not dress all the 'extravagant children of his fantasy' into words that found their way into print. It is also to be borne in mind that poets are not moved to write of all of their experiences. As his friend and editor of his works, Rodriguez Correa, says in the prologue to the fourth edition of Becquer's complete works in 1877, "The Rimas of Becquer are not the total expression of a poet, but rather what is known of a poet."

Becquer's niece, Julia, has left an account of childhood in the Becquer household and of the pleasant memories of her uncle, Gustavo Adolfo, and his children. He would go to great lengths to amuse them, playing music, telling stories, making up puppet shows, etc., and sharing in their delight; yet not one of his Rimas deals with the joys of fatherhood. Shall we assume then, that these were not meaningful experiences for him?

If there is a dimension of Becquer that is not revealed in his work, there is, on the other hand, in what is known of his life, ample substance for the sadness in many of the Rimas.

Becquer was born in Seville on February 17, 1836, the fourth in a family of eight sons, not all of whom survived infancy. His father, Jose Dominguez Insausti (Vequer), a painter of some reknown, died when Gustavo was only five. The surname, Becquer, had been adopted from that of his noble Flemish forebears, who had settled in Seville in the latter part of the sixteenth century. Gustavo's mother, Joaquina Bastida, is also said to have been of noble parentage. In 1846, she placed her son in the Colegio de San Telmo, a school that prepared orphaned boys, at no cost, for a career at sea, provided they were of noble descent. The following year, Becquer's mother died. Also, the school was closed by the government.

We can perhaps imagine the traumatic effect of these tragedies on the psyche of a sensitive boy of eleven. The elements that shaped his life up to that time can be seen in his later work. There is the preoccupation with death, the inconsolable longing for love, the escape sought in the sea (Rima 35, "Giant waves that roaring break/on far off beaches and lonely dunes... Take me with you!), the imagery of the 'heraldic crest' (Rima 3), and the Gothic tone of the Leyendas. Of course, many of these themes are also to be found in the Romantic literature of the time, but it is clear that they touched a fertile imagination that could easily relate to them with all the depth of his soul.

Given the artistic environment into which he was born, and whatever talents he might have inherited, a noble name of Germanic origin, the loss of his father and mother in his tender years; Becquer would seem almost to have been destined to write as he did. Yet his brothers also shared this heritage, and, of these, none expressed themselves in literature, though Valeriano, to whom he was closest in age and temperament, did become a painter. What precise factors of age, environment, or genes contributed to this distinction by Gustavo Adolfo, we do not know, but fortuitous circumstance represented by his god-mother, Dona Manuela Monnehay, assisted in his development as a writer. This cultured and generous lady, who was childless, took him into her home upon the death of his mother, and there, having her ample library at his disposal, he became acquainted with the works of Chateaubriand, Victor Hugo, Musset, Byron, Hoffmann, and other masters of early nineteenth century romanticism. He read the Odes of Horace in translation and was inspired to study Latin. His reading of the poetry of Zorilla inspired him to imitate the life style of the author of Don Juan Tenorio. Thus, at eighteen, against his god-mother's wishes, he left for Madrid with the dream of attaining literary fame and fortune.

There, he suffered the disillusionment and poverty usually associated with the Bohemian concept of the struggling artist's life. He sought in the theater a more lucrative and immediate acclaim, writing and adapting plays in collaboration with Garcia Luna, a young writer like himself. These had rather short runs and were severely criticized by the press. In 1857, he became quite ill, and it is said that this period marks a turning point in his work. The first of his 'leyendas' to be published appeared in May of 1858. Also, a good number of the 'rimas' were written during his convalescence. One of these is Rima 45 (LXI) in which we see his loneliness and despair.

> "On seeing my hours of fever
> and sleeplessness slowly tread,
> who will come to sit
> at the edge of my lonely bed?

During the period of recuperation from his illness, Becquer was fond of taking walks through the streets of Madrid. Legend has it that on one such walk, he saw on the balcony of her home, Julia Espin, the daughter of the director of the orchestra of the Teatro Real, and niece of the composer, Rossini. The worlds in which they lived were far apart and it is doubtful that he ever openly declared to her his love. Becquer's niece was named after Julia, and in an interview with someone who was doing a study on Becquer, she states that Julia Espin was the muse of the Rimas. An intimate friend of

Becquer, Julio Nombela, claimed that she was the inspiration of all the rimas of love, but this is rejected by most of his contemporary biographers because the depth of passion and bitterness in them does not seem to correspond to their relationship.

In 1928, Fernando Iglesias Figueroa published three letters from Becquer to his friend Rodriguez Correa, and another by the latter to a mutual friend, which make reference to Elisa Guillen. Little is known about her, but these letters dated from December 1859 to March 1861 reveal a deep emotional crisis. In Becquer's last letter, he speaks of burning letters, relics of his former life, "of the hours that will never return," a phrase which reminds us of Rima LIII (38). He imagines seeing a hand rise from the flames, a hand which mocks him, and which resembles her hand, 'today probably being held by someone else'.

Shortly afterwards he met and married Casta Esteban, the daughter of a doctor. It is claimed by Casta's detractors, such as Becquer's niece, Julia, that he futilely sought in this marriage, refuge from the loneliness and disappointment he had suffered until then. In Rima 93 dedicated to Casta, he says, "You lend new life and hope/ to a heart already dead to love"; According to a study by Heliodoro Carpintero of Becquer's life with Casta in Soria, their early married life was a tranquil one in which he continued to write and earn a living from his writing. This biographer believes that it was the presence of Gustavo's brother, Valeriano, that disturbed the home. Valeriano, Julia's father, was a restless spirit; he had separated from his wife and was engaged in painting genre scenes of the different provinces of Spain. He influenced Gustavo to accompany him, so they could work together, painter and poet. Shortly after his return from one such excursion with Valeriano, Casta gave birth to their third son. It was rumored that this son was not his, and so Gustavo left his wife taking the two older boys with him. He lived for a year with Valeriano and his daughter in Toledo, suffering poverty once again, but now with added responsibilities. The situation improved in 1870, when he returned to Madrid to assume the literary directorship of a new magazine, La Ilustracion de Madrid. Valeriano was to provide artwork for it. But the hopes for the beginning of a new life in the new decade vanished with death of Valeriano in September of 1870. Casta returned to Madrid to comfort her husband, but it was too late. Gustavo died in December of 1870 at the age of thirty four.

The Rimas

Tragedy surrounds even the publication of these short poems. A number of them had appeared in magazines during his lifetime, and an admiring patron, Luis Gonzales Bravo, an important political figure of the time, had agreed to pay for the cost of publishing a collection of the Rimas. The manuscript was destroyed, however, when the latter's house was sacked during the political upheaval of 1866. Becquer rewrote them from memory and, shortly before his death, presented them to his childhood friend, Narciso Campillo, with the request that he edit them as he saw fit. His devoted friends, struggling painters and poets like himself, included them in a posthumous edition of his complete works in 1871.

The order given to the Rimas by Narciso Campillo is a thematic one: Rimas I - XI deal with poetry; XII - XXIX, love; XXX - LI, disillusionment; LII - LXXVI, despair, loneliness and death. Because of this order, critics had at one time, believed that the Rimas reflect the tempestuous course of a love affair. There is a sequential development in the love poems, beginning with poems of encounter, the dawning of romance, the ecstasy of fulfillment, the discovery of deception, and ending in a longing for death. Much research has been done in order to determine whether this sequence parallels his affair with Julia Espin or Elisa Guillen. Carpintero, mentioned above, believes that it was Becquer's wife Casta who provided the inspiration for much of his work, including also the Cartas literarias a una mujer. There can be no doubt that there are rimas inspired by Julia, Elisa, and

Casta. However, one should also take into account what Becquer says in the Introduction sinfonica, "my heart is divided between phantoms of my imagination and real people; my memory records the confused names and dates of women and days that have died or passed, with days and women who have never existed except in my mind."

The order given the Rimas by Becquer himself, the order in which they are presented in this volume, does not follow a thematic sequence. Becquer's original manuscript, entitled, Libro de los gorriones, which is found in the Biblioteca Nacional of Madrid, begins with the Introduccion sinfonica. This is followed by an unfinished story and then by five hundred pages left blank for the inclusion of other literary works projected by Becquer. On page 529, there appears an index to the Rimas, which is followed by Rimas 1 to 76. The remainder of the rimas in this translation are those which have been subsequently collected by scholars and which appear in the Aguado edition of his complete works published in Madrid in 1949. This edition follows the order in the Libro de los gorriones (swallows), Becquer's manuscript.

I have also chosen to follow the order indicated by Becquer, for to begin with, it is Becquer's order, and, though we can only guess at the reasoning behind it, it is clear that he intended them to be presented in this sequence, and that he probably had some reason for it. To me the Rimas, as Becquer arranged them, resemble a piece of music opening with an atomal chord, a dissonance that strikes the heart. Rimas 1 to 4 deal with the pain of love lost, the first of this series being the most intense. As we go on, the dominant theme is still despair, but it is interspersed with thoughts on poetry (Rima 7, 11, 13). Even a more pleasant poem of love is included in this beginning, Rima 6, which describes a flower sleeping on a woman's breast. The longing for death is introduced in Rima 1 which deals of love's despair. Thus, we see a fusion of themes, which is consistent with the thoughts expressed by Becquer in the <u>Cartas literarias a una mujer</u> on the oneness of beauty, love, and religion.

The subtle effects and musicality of the rimas are achieved, in the main, by the use of assonant rhyme. In this technique, which is seldom used in English poetry, the rhyme depends on the sound of the last accented vowel in a line of verse, and whatever vowel sounds may follow. Intervening consonant sounds are disregarded. This allows the poet a wider selection of words and avoids the obvious and repetitious ring of consonant rhyme. Also, since the stress is on the harmony of the vowel sounds, the reader is left with whatever subliminal feelings the sound may evoke in him. For example, the rhyming of the word 'time' with 'tide', an example of assonance since the dissimilar consonants 'm' and 'd' are disregarded, leaves the listener with the repeated sound of the 'i', phonetically 'ai', which sounds somewhat like a sigh (which would also rhyme with 'time' and 'tide') and lends to the mournful tone of the poem. Since this is one of the dominant features of Becquer's versification, it has also been applied in the translation.

Becquer has left a lasting influence on Spanish poetry, an influence that has been openly acknowledged by some of the most successful and more widely acclaimed writers in Spanish and Spanish-American literature. It is my hope that through this translation, completed one hundred years after his death, he will become better known and appreciated by the English reading public.

ACKNOWLEDGEMENT

In preparing this addendum to my translation, I have relied most heavily on the following works:

Becquer, Gustavo Adolfo. Rimas, ed. Clasicos Caste-
  llanos. Madrid, Espasa-Calpe, 1963.

Becquer, Gustavo Adolfo. Obras completas de Gustavo
  Adolfo Becquer. Madrid, ed. Afrodisio Aguado, 1949.

Brown, Rica. Becquer. Barcelona, ed. Aedos, 1963.

Carpintero, Heliodoro. Becquer de par en par. Madrid,
  1957.

Diaz, Jose Pedro. G.A. Becquer: Vida y poesia, 2nd ed.
  Madrid, 1958.